GUIDE TO STANDARDIZED DRUMSET NOTATION

DEDICATION

This project would not have been possible without the encouragement and support of my wife, Nancy, and my daughters, Jennifer and Kimberly. I will be forever grateful for their love.

ACKNOWLEDGEMENTS

A sincere thank you to all my teachers through the years: George Boberg, Gerald Carlyss, George Gaber, William Roberts, Ben Udell, Gary Werdesheim, Charmaine Asher Wiley, and William Zickos. Another thank you must be given to my students, past and present—you are now my teachers.

A special thanks to Rick Mattingly for his expert editing of this book and Shawn Brown for her creative layout and design.

GUIDE TO STANDARDIZED DRUMSET NOTATION

by
Norman Weinberg

Copyright © 1998 by the Percussive Arts Society, Inc.

ISBN 0-9664928-1-1

International Copyright Secured. All Rights Reserved.

No part of this publication may be reproduced or transmitted in any form
or by any means, electronic or mechanical, including photocopy, recording,
or any information storage and retrieval system, without permission in writing
from the publisher.

Percussive Arts Society, Inc.
701 N.W. Ferris Ave.
Lawton, Oklahoma 73507, USA

Library of Congress Catalog Card Number 98-66737

Printed in the United States of America
98 99 00 01 SP 9 8 7 6 5 4 3 2 1

TABLE OF CONTENTS

FOREWORD		vi
PREFACE		vii
THE NEED FOR STANDARDIZATION		viii
THE GUIDELINE		xi
1	GENERAL NOTATION	1
2	DRUMS	9
3	CYMBALS	11
4	NOTEHEADS	15
5	ARTICULATIONS	19
6	VOICING	27
7	LEGEND	31
8	IMPROVISATIONAL NOTATION	33
BIBLIOGRAPHY		41
ABOUT THE AUTHOR		43

FOREWORD

One of the biggest challenges for anyone attempting to notate a drumset part is that there is no absolute "standard" in terms of what makes up a drumset. One can generally assume that it will include a bass drum, snare drum, two or three tom-toms, a ride cymbal, a crash cymbal and a pair of hi-hat cymbals. But some drummers use less than that while many drummers use a lot more.

Perhaps it is the non-consistency of the drumset itself that has led to so many variations in the systems that have been used to notate written parts for the instrument. Nevertheless, certain practices have become relatively standardized over the years and most drumset players recognize a somewhat consistent arrangement of basic drumset components on a standard music staff.

But the more instruments involved, the more the lack of a standardized system becomes obvious in the published literature. In order to arrive at the guidelines presented in this text, Norm Weinberg analyzed over 200 published works involving notated drumset parts, including instructional books, arrangements and compositions. By building on the most commonly used approaches to drumset notation, Weinberg has created a notational system that allows just about any drumset to be clearly notated on a five-line staff using standard, understandable musical notation.

In the preparation of this book, the material was reviewed by a number of drumset performers, educators and music-publishing professionals who are authorities on drumset performance and notation, including members of the Percussive Arts Society Publications Committee (Dave Black, Alfred Music; Michael Finkelstein, Warner Bros. Music; Garwood Whaley, Meredith Music; and myself, Hal Leonard Corporation and *Modern Drummer* magazine) and members of the PAS Drumset Committee (Ed Soph, University of North Texas; and Bob Breithaupt, Capital University).

The Percussive Arts Society hopes that the guidelines contained herein will aid performers, teachers, students, composers, arrangers, orchestrators and music engravers in producing clear drumset parts for a variety of uses. While it would be impossible to cover every possible arrangement of instruments that a drumset could encompass, these guidelines cover the majority of situations and provide basic principles to help people arrive at logical solutions to unique circumstances.

—*Rick Mattingly*

PREFACE

A logical and consistent notational system for the drumset has finally arrived.

How should one notate music for the drumset? This seems a simple question, yet an examination of the published resource materials and performance literature reveals that composers, arrangers, authors, editors and educators often embrace different views on the subject. This book answers the question by codifying the notational symbols and procedures used for drumset performance.

This guideline does not suggest a unique or new notational system for the drumset. Instead, it presents a clarification, simplification and amplification (when required) of the notational systems already in use in a majority of the published literature.

Recent history offers two examples of attempts to codify a language. Esperanto was an effort to create an international spoken and written language that would be used by all the peoples of the earth. MIDI is a computer protocol that enables electronic musical instruments to communicate with other computer-based systems. Esperanto was a failure, MIDI a success. The success or failure of any codified system rests on the desire to adopt a standard without regard to special interests or personal views.

In an effort to avoid special interests and biases when compiling the guidelines contained in this book, the notational systems of 220 performance works and reference texts were analyzed in great detail. Reference and performance materials were further divided into two categories: those works that employ precise notation (compositions, magazine articles, method books, style guides, etc.) and those based on improvisatory frameworks (drumset charts for contemporary music).

This is a guidebook for the composer, arranger, performer, author, educator and editor who needs a notational system for the drumset that will be clear, concise and understood by the drumming community. Only when the composer and performer understand the same language can true communication take place. Frank McCarty wrote that the main goal of a standardized notation

> ...is to strengthen the notational language between composers and performers by simplifying and clarifying its content and standardizing its applicability without, however, limiting its potential for expansion.[1]

---

[1] Frank McCarty, "Percussion Notation," *Percussionist* 15 (Winter 1978): 50.

THE NEED FOR STANDARDIZATION

Musical notation is a fascinating topic. Its long history has been charged with dynamic developments, exotic systems, and a passion for blending the two dichotomies of simplicity and precision. Virginia Gaburo stated the importance of notation on our musical experience when she wrote:

> Notation's benefits for the facilitation of musical idea manipulation have been immense, not only for the achievement of theoretical and analytical objectives, but for the achievement of compositional ones as well.[1]

While the purpose for using a musical notation may be obvious, the notation's meaning itself is not always so apparent. All communication systems require convention, and musical notation is no exception. In order for communication to take place, the speaker must use a language familiar to the listener. One might assume that the composer and performer approach the language of drumset notation with the same notion of what is implied. Yet this common understanding between composer and performer often breaks down, leaving the performer confused concerning the exact intent of the composer.

When discussing notational problems that create confusion for performers, Hugo Cole offers the following list of the eight most common causes of problematic notation:

1. Graphical faults (poor spacing and alignment, badly-formed symbols, unclear layout).

2. Inconsistency (contradictory markings, symbols used in different senses without good cause).

3. Too little information given (that is, too little for adequate performance under the prevailing conditions).

    > The most treacherous situation of all is that of the generally consistent writer who abandons consistency. If, for instance, *nearly* all simultaneous notes are properly aligned, the few exceptions will be much more likely to mislead than if alignment was haphazard throughout.

4. Too much information given (that is, unnecessarily much under prevailing conditions).

5. Meaningless precision.

    > ... unnecessary instructions such as fingerings for expert players or bowings on every note are unnecessary in all conceivable contexts, and so unjustifiable. Excessive use of redundant and precautionary markings is also a symptom of overanxiety, and is to be deprecated.

6. Uncertainty as to terms of contract (degree of latitude to be taken in interpretation).

7. Ambiguity (where signs may have two meanings, only one of which can be right).

8. Insufficiency of notation for the job at hand.[2]

Percussion notation has its own unique set of problems. As composers and arrangers invent signs, symbols and terminology, the percussionist is faced with learning a multitude of musical languages.

During the course of research for this book, a startling number of notational variations were found, including staff systems ranging from no lines to ten lines. An amazing assortment of noteheads and articulations were discovered in the literature: ninety-one individual notehead variations and sixty-four different articulations. Certainly, such diversity is not necessary!

The wide variety of notational procedures encountered in drumset notation can cause frustration for the novice and experienced player alike. No other instrument in traditional ensemble organizations asks a musician to work within such a disorganized and ever-changing notational system.

Creation of a standardized percussion notation has long been the wish of performers and composers. Yet, the dream has not materialized. Many years have passed since Frank McCarty's questionnaire on percussion notation was published by the Percussive Arts Society. The results of the questionnaire proved that 87% of the respondents agreed with the statement that "an international symbology should be adopted."[3] And, Donald Martino sums up the desire to clarify notation by saying "the need to clarify and standardize the existing symbols of our notation must surely be evident."[4]

Recently, there has been an explosion of drumset literature. An increase in the popularity of jazz, pop and rock music (all of which make strong use of the drumset) continues to produce more musicians who are interested in learning to play the drumset. These musicians are a potential market for publishers who produce books and materials for drumset instruction as well as written arrangements of recorded performances. The emergence of journals and popular magazines dedicated to a large extent toward drumset performance practices has produced additional exercises and transcriptions of recorded drumset performances. The increased influence of Latin, Caribbean, African and other world music upon the commercial music scene has spawned a variety of "style" and technical guides for the drumset. The evolution of the home-publishing industry has made it possible for anyone with a new idea to publish a method book, arrangement or musical composition.

In the present state of affairs, each method book, performance transcription, style study, magazine article or musical composition requires a new and individual solution to the problem of drumset notation, and drumset notation falls into further disarray.

The notational system presented in this guideline will suffice for the vast majority of current drumset music. As drumset performance requirements advance past their current point, this guideline can be expanded to fit the needs of both the composer and performer.

If all composers, arrangers, editors and publishers adopt the guideline presented here, many aspects of drumset performance would be enhanced. They would be performing a great service to the drumset musicians who are expected to properly interpret their creations.

---

[1] Virginia Gaburo, *Notation (a lecture to be performed by solo speaker to attentive audience)* (La Jolla, CA.: Lingua Press, 1977), 43.

[2] Hugo Cole, *Sounds and Signs: Aspects of Musical Notation* (London: Oxford University Press, 1974), 32–33.

[3] Frank McCarty, "Percussion Notation," *Percussionist* 15 (Winter 1978): 57–58.

[4] John C. O'Neill, "Recent Trends in Percussion Notation," *Percussionist* 18 (Fall 1980): 51.

THE GUIDELINE

Drumset performance can be divided into two distinct styles: precise and improvisational. Precise musical performances are essential for many drumset solos, percussion ensembles, method books and educational articles. Improvisational performances are indispensable for popular music. Since these two performance styles have distinct notational requirements, this guideline will be divided into two parts. The first will cover notational guidelines for precise performance notation. The second will present guidelines for improvisational performance notation.

In arriving at the recommendations for this guideline, the criteria for selection employed by the International Conference on New Music Notation were constantly consulted. The Conference's criteria were:

1. Given a choice, the preferable notation is the one that is an extension of traditional notation.

2. The notation should lend itself to immediate recognition. This means it should be:

    a. graphically distinct

    b. as self-explanatory as possible

3. Proposals should be made only in cases where a sufficient need is anticipated.

4. Analogous procedures in different instrumental families should be notated similarly.

5. Given a choice, the preferable notation is the one that has received relatively wide acceptance.

6. The notation should be sufficiently distinct graphically to permit a reasonable amount of distortion due to variations in handwriting and different writing implements.

7. The notation used should be the most efficient for the organizational principles that underlie the respective composition.

8. Given a choice, the preferable notation is the one that is spatially economical.[1]

Specifically applied to this guideline, criteria one and five were interpreted to mean that a preferable notation is one that is employed in a majority of the 220 publications examined. Criterion two ("graphically distinct") specifies that signs and symbols should not contradict one another. In other words, each notation recommendation must represent a unique sign, a unique staff position and/or a unique symbol. Criterion three suggests that recommendations not be made for performance techniques of a highly individual nature. And criterion six was expanded to include notational symbols that are common to computer-based music notation software.

---

[1] Herman Sabbe, Kurt Stone, and Gerald Warfield, eds., "International Conference on New Musical Notation Report," Interface 4 (November 1975): 33.

1
GENERAL NOTATION

THE STAFF
It is recommended that all drumset music be notated on the traditional five-line staff.

THE CLEF
All music for drumset should employ the "neutral clef" (sometimes called the "percussion clef") to indicate that staff positions are not indicative of precise pitch. There are two common visual symbols for this clef. Either version is acceptable, but the first version is preferred.

Neutral Clef (Preferred version)

Neutral Clef

BARLINES
The double barline (two thin vertical lines) should appear whenever there is a change of tempo, and between major sections of a work to provide indications of structural divisions.

The final barline (composed of one thin and one thick line) should appear only at the end of a movement or an entire composition.

Barlines

REPEAT BARS

The one-bar repeat indicates that the previous measure is repeated. This sign can be used several times in series, but should not be used at the beginning of a line. When four or more repeat bars are used in succession, a small parenthetical number should be placed above selected repeat signs to indicate the total number of statements of the pattern. In most cases, numbering every fourth or eighth bar is sufficient.

One Bar Repeat

The two-bar repeat indicates that the previous two measures are repeated. This sign can be used several times in succession, but should not be used at the beginning of a line.

Two Bar Repeat

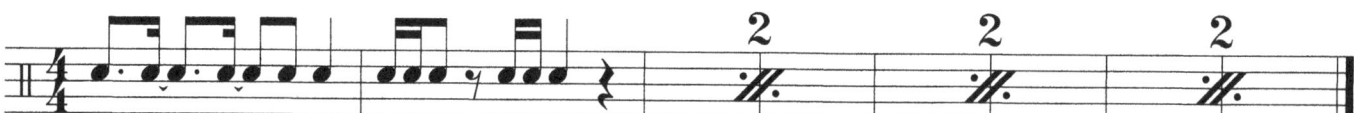

SLASH NOTATION

Slash notation is used to indicate that the player is to improvise a part in the appropriate style. Often, a suggested time feel and instrumentation are notated in the first bar and slashes are then used to indicate that the player should continue in the same style. A written instruction should be included above the staff to indicate whether the drummer is to play a timekeeping pattern, a fill or a solo in measures that contain slashes.

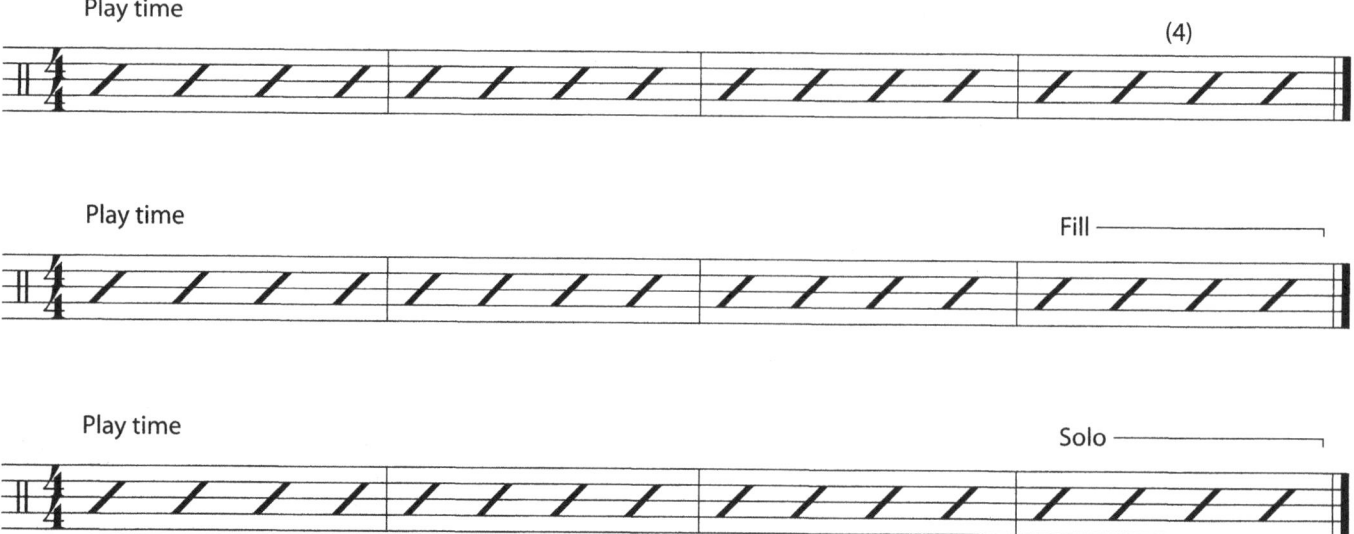

RHYTHMIC NOTATION

Rhythmic notation indicates that the player is expected to play the indicated rhythm. The player is free to choose the instrumentation.

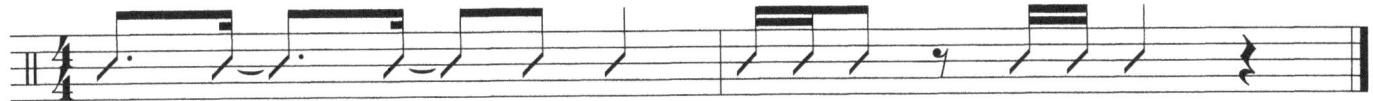

STEM DIRECTION FOR ONE-VOICE NOTATION

Drumset notation evolved from notation for snare drum and bass drum in which snare drum is written on the third space with stems up and bass drum is written on the first space with stems down. Even if there is no bass drum part, solo snare drum parts are typically written stems up.

"Linear" timekeeping parts and those in which all voices share the same stems (and beams) are typically written stems up. This is most common when it may be more clear to the performer how certain rhythms played with the feet correspond to the rhythms played in the hands.

Linear Notation

Stems Up Notation

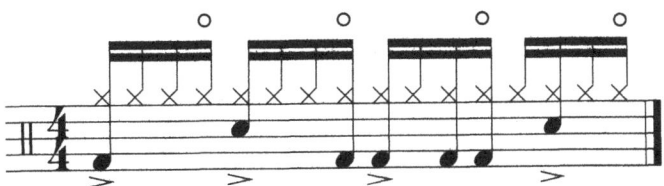

When a clear distinction between hands and feet will result in a more understandable presentation for the performer, the instruments played by the hands are written exclusively with up stems while the instruments played with the feet are written exclusively with down stems.

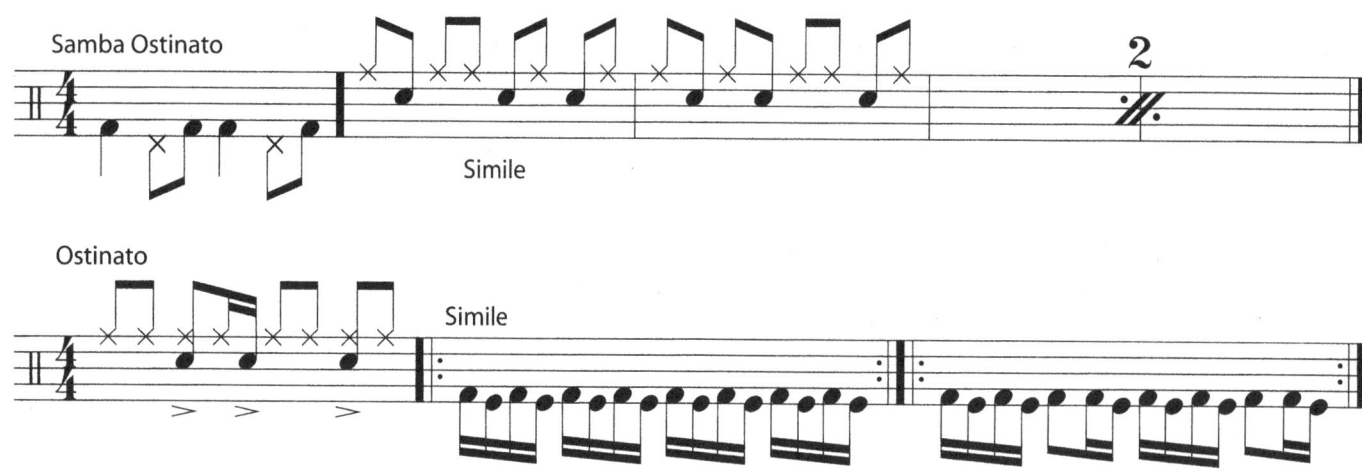

In situations where the drumset is functioning more as a multiple-percussion setup and playing "melodic" patterns, rather than as a single instrument playing timekeeping patterns, it is appropriate to follow standard practices for stem direction. In such cases, single, non-beamed notes that lie below the third line of the staff should be written stems up. Single notes written on or above the third line should be written stems down. When non-beamed multiple notes share a stem, the direction should be determined by the note furthest from the third line of the staff. If the outside notes are equidistant from the third line, the stem should go down. When several notes are beamed together, the note(s) furthest from the third line determines the direction. If the outside notes are equidistant from the third line, the stem should go down.

Single Stems

Chord Stems

Beams

Cue notes are generally stemmed in the direction opposite from normal.

See Chapter 6: VOICING, for further discussion and examples of stem-direction options.

GRACE NOTES

Single grace notes (flams) should be written with a single flag—similar to eighth notes. An oblique slash should cross both the stem and the flag of a single grace note. Groups of two or more grace notes (drags or ruffs) should be written with two beams (similar to sixteenth notes). Typically, percussion notation does not use the slash for two or more grace notes. Grace notes should be slurred into the primary note. All grace notes should be written with their stems up, regardless of where the notes are placed on the staff.

Snare Flam

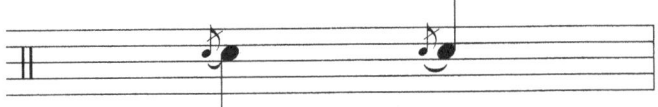

Tom Flam

Snare Drag

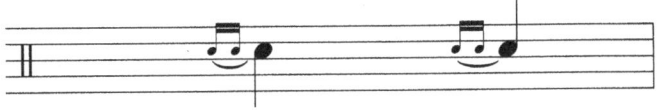

STEM DIRECTION WITH TWO VOICES

The above rules for stem direction are altered when there are two separate voices on a single staff. In all cases, the upper voice should be stemmed up while the lower voice is stemmed down regardless of their position on the staff. This applies to single notes, multiple notes, beamed notes and grace notes.

Single Notes

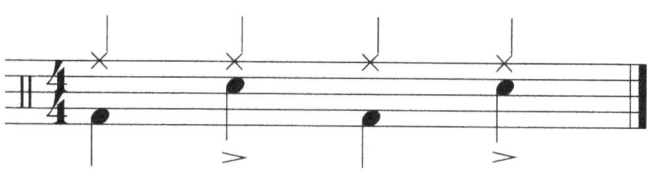

Multiple Notes

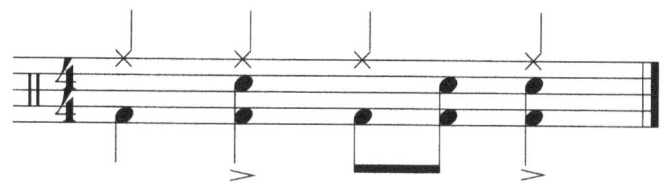

Beamed Notes

Grace Notes—Two Voices

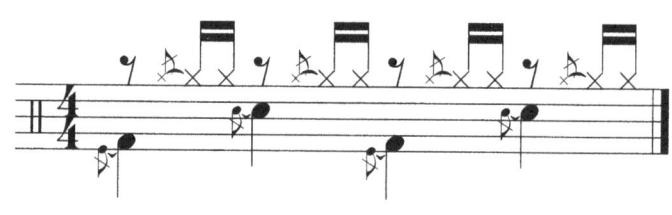

RHYTHMIC ABBREVIATIONS

An abbreviation consists of a note with one or more oblique slashes drawn through the stem, or centered above or below a whole note. The note indicates the total duration of the abbreviation and the slashes indicate the note values of the abbreviation.

ROLLS

Rolls are commonly written as abbreviated thirty-second notes in all but the slowest tempi.

SPACING

Traditionally, music is spaced so that longer note values have more space after them than shorter note values. However, notes are spaced proportionally rather than mathematically; e.g., a quarter note has more space after it than an eighth note, but not twice as much.

But with most multi-voice drumset music, especially patterns contained in method books geared towards younger students, the music should be spaced mathematically so that a voice that is supposed to be played very evenly (such as a ride pattern or bass drum pulse) is evenly spaced.

Mathematical Spacing

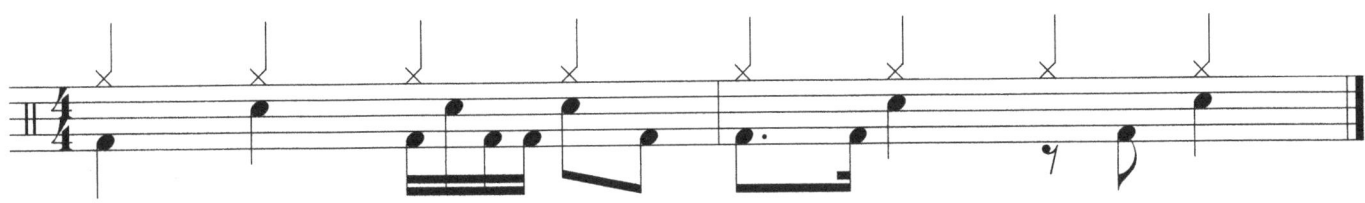

Proportional Spacing

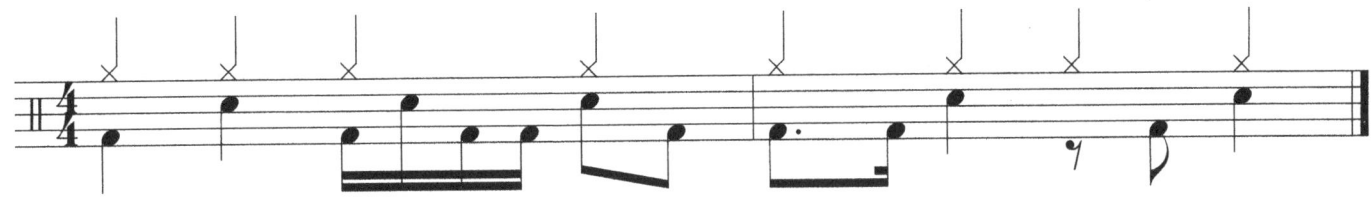

2
DRUMS

The following guidelines discuss notehead positioning only. For discussions of stem direction, see Chapter 1: GENERAL NOTATION and Chapter 6: VOICING.

SNARE DRUM
The snare drum should be written on the third space of the staff.

Snare Drum

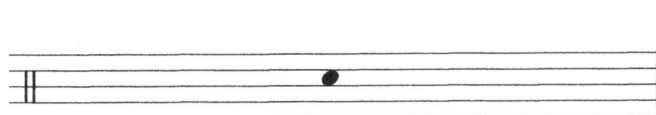

BASS DRUM #1
Works calling for a single bass drum should place this instrument on the first space of the staff.

Bass Drum #1

BASS DRUM #2
When a second bass drum is required, it should be scored on the first line of the staff.

Bass Drum #2

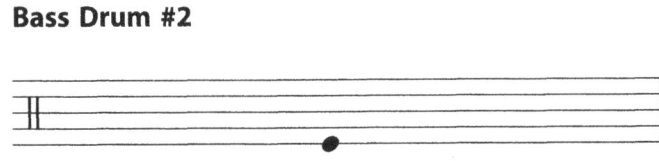

TOM-TOMS
The staff position for tom-toms depends upon the total number of toms required for performance. The most typical drumset configurations include two or three toms.

If certain types (single- or double-headed) or sizes (12", 13", 16") of tom-toms are required, their descriptions should be given in the legend and no additional indication is necessary in the music.

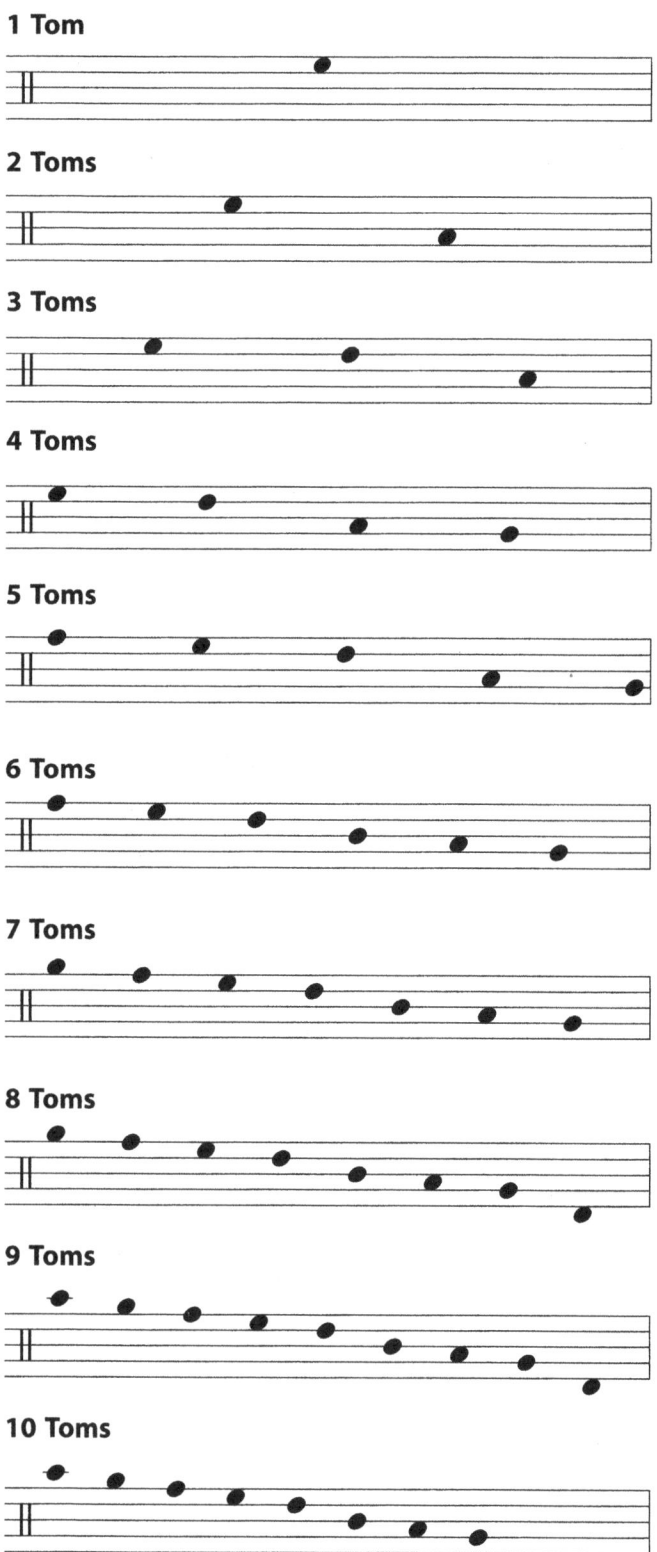

3
CYMBALS

The following guidelines discuss notehead positioning only. For discussions of stem direction, see Chapter 1: GENERAL NOTATION and Chapter 6: VOICING.

NOTEHEADS

Cymbals (including hi-hats) should be written with "X" noteheads. Sans-serif X noteheads are preferred, but serif X's (such as the "double sharp" X) are acceptable. However, serif and sans-serif noteheads should not be mixed in the same composition. When note values of a half-note or greater are necessary, the notehead should be an open diamond. (See Chapter 4: NOTEHEADS.)

HI-HAT WITH HANDS

When the hi-hat is to be played with sticks, brushes or mallets, notes should be written on the first space above the staff.

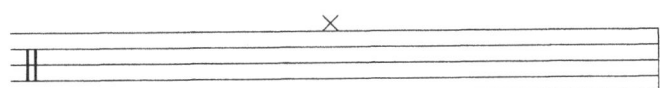

HI-HAT WITH FOOT

When the hi-hat is to be played with the foot pedal, notes should be written on the first space below the staff.

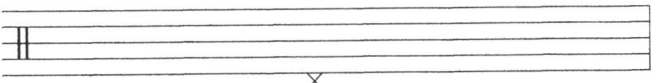

HI-HAT #2

Some drummers use two hi-hats. The second hi-hat is usually kept in the closed position and is not controlled by a foot pedal. Notes for the second hi-hat should be written on the fourth space of the staff.

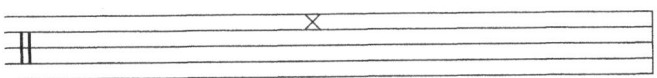

RIDE CYMBAL #1

This guide recommends that the ride cymbal be written on the top line of the staff. This staff position provides a clear distinction between notes to be played on the hi-hat cymbals and those to be played on the ride cymbal.

Note that in some drumset charts for rock, jazz and popular music, the ride is notated in the same position as the hi-hat (first space above the staff), as the composer or arranger has no preference for instrument, and players are then free to choose between ride cymbal and hi-hat at will. The disadvantage of this style of notation is that when differentiation is desired, additional text expressions are required.

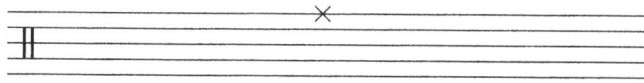

RIDE CYMBAL #2

When a second ride cymbal is required, it should be notated on the fourth line of the staff.

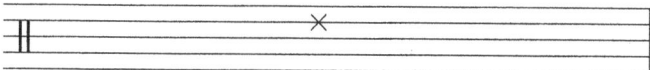

CRASH CYMBAL #1

The crash cymbal should be written on the first ledger line above the staff.

CRASH CYMBAL #2

When an additional crash cymbal is needed, it should be written on the space above the first ledger line above the staff.

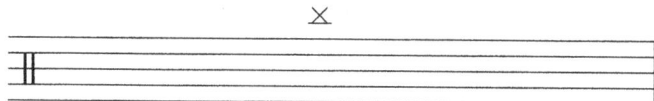

CRASH CYMBAL #3

When a composition requires three different crash cymbals, the third cymbal should be written on the second ledger line above the staff.

ADDITIONAL CYMBALS

If more cymbals are required for the performance, the additional cymbals should be placed above the second ledger line.

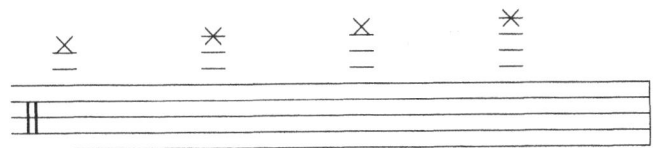

CYMBAL CLASSIFICATION

If desired, the exact cymbal types (China, splash, sizzle, swish, etc.) and sizes (12", 16", 22") can be identified in the legend of the composition. For the performer, the fact that a cymbal written at a certain staff location is a China cymbal or splash cymbal is not relevant. Once the instrument is identified in the legend, and the player places the requested instrument at a convenient physical location for performance, a written identification of the type of cymbal outside the legend is not necessary.

4
NOTEHEADS

CYMBAL NOTEHEADS

Cymbals (including hi-hats) should be written with "X" noteheads. Sans-serif X noteheads are preferred, but serif Xs (such as the "double sharp" X) are acceptable. However, serif and sans-serif noteheads should not be mixed in the same composition. When note values of a half-note or greater are necessary, the notehead should be an open diamond.

Sans-serif cymbal noteheads

Serif cymbal noteheads

DRUMS AND CYMBALS SHARING A STAFF POSITION

The use of X noteheads provides a method of placing both a drum and a cymbal at the same staff position.

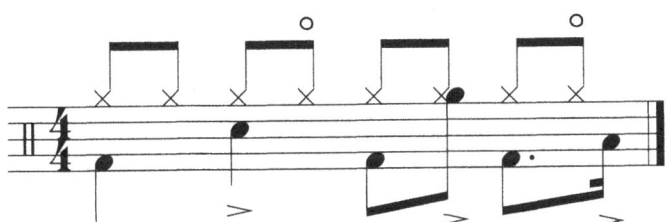

COWBELL NOTEHEADS

When a cowbell is incorporated into a drumset, it can be written on the same staff with a triangle-shaped notehead to distinguish it from drum and cymbal notation. This allows placement on the fourth space of the staff. Solid (filled) noteheads should be used for values of a quarter note or smaller; open (non-filled) noteheads should be used for values of half or whole notes.

In general percussion notation, cowbells are indicated with standard noteheads. If a separate staff is being used for many additional instruments, normal noteheads are suggested.

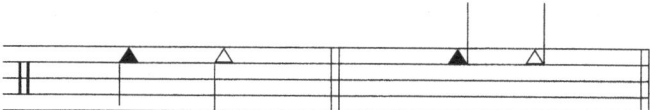

GHOST STROKE NOTEHEADS

Ghost strokes are notes that are played at an extremely soft dynamic level. Ghost strokes should be written with parenthetical noteheads. Ghost strokes can be effective on any instrument of the drumset.

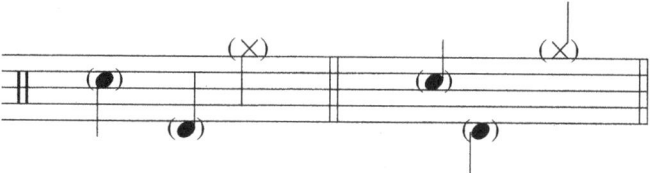

RIMSHOT AND CROSS-STICK NOTEHEADS

Some composers and arrangers have indicated rimshots with the X notehead. This is problematic for a number of reasons. There are several different types of rimshots and each main type has a number of subtle variations. Use of the X notehead affords no method of delineating one technique or variation from the other without the use of text expressions. By using X noteheads, some tom-tom rimshots would be impossible to distinguish from notes intended for cymbals. It is unnecessary to use one set of symbols for rimshots on the snare drum and another for rimshots on the tom-toms. This guideline recommends using precise indications for the rimshot and the cross-stick.

Rimshot: The standard rimshot is performed with a single stroke in which the tip of the drumstick contacts the head at the same time the shaft of the stick comes down against the rim. The indication for this type of rimshot is a notehead with a backslash. This technique is most often used on the snare drum but can also be used on tom-toms.

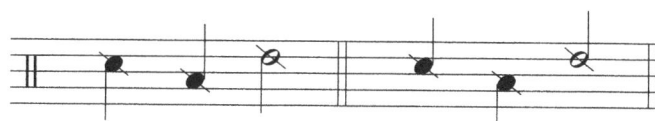

Cross-Stick: The cross-stick technique is performed by resting the tip of the stick on the drumhead and then bringing the shaft of the stick down on the drum's counterhoop. This effect is often used in beat patterns of Afro-Cuban/Latin music to simulate the sound of claves. The indication of the cross-stick technique should be a circled notehead. This technique is most often used on the snare drum but can also be used on tom-toms.

Rimshot Variations: While many rimshot techniques and variations are common in musical performance, they are so rarely notated that no common symbology has yet emerged.

Additional rimshot styles such as the rim click (the stick strikes only the rim without making contact with the head of the drum), the stickshot (performed by resting one stick's tip on the drumhead and striking that stick with the other stick), or striking the shell of the drum (similar to cascara playing on timbales) should be notated by creating a new notehead and/or articulation symbol, and clearly defining the symbology and playing technique in the legend. Once the techniques and symbols are defined in the legend, they should be strictly followed throughout the composition.

NOTEHEADS FOR ADDITIONAL INSTRUMENTS

Composers occasionally score for instruments that are not always associated with the normal drumset (such as woodblock, gong, tambourine, triangle, temple blocks, etc). When additional instruments are notated in drumset music, they can use triangle-shaped noteheads (either solid or open, depending on the durational value) to allow for their placement within a single five-line staff. The use of triangle-shaped noteheads permits these instruments to share staff positions with drums and cymbals. Instructions for the use of additional instruments must be included in the legend and strictly observed throughout the composition.

In cases where so many additional percussion instruments are being used that it is impractical to include them on the same staff, a separate staff should be used for the instruments that are not considered part of the normal drumset, and standard noteheads should be used.

Double Stave Notation (Key)

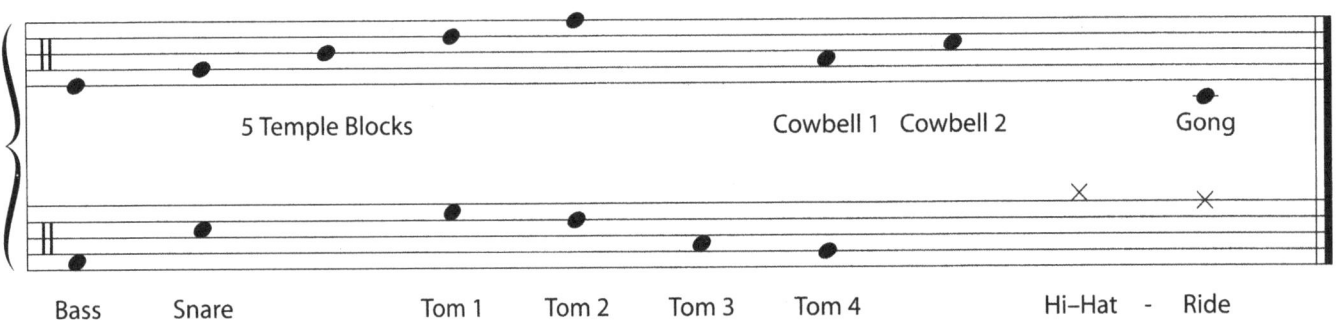

Double Stave Notation (Example)

5
ARTICULATIONS

ARTICULATION POSITIONS

Generally speaking, only the musical articulations of staccato (a dot) and tenuto (a dash) are placed inside the staff in single-voice music. All other articulations should be placed outside of the staff.

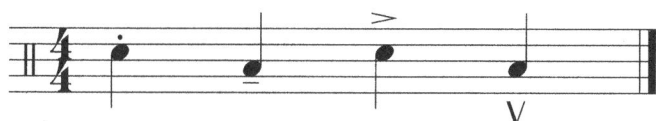

Music written in a single voice with both upstem and downstem notes has articulation signs placed over or under the notehead rather than the stem. However, in single-line drum music in which all stems are up it is common to have articulations placed on the stem side of the note. Stickings, however, are placed under the staff (see page 25).

In two-voice notation, articulation signs are always placed on the stem side of the note.

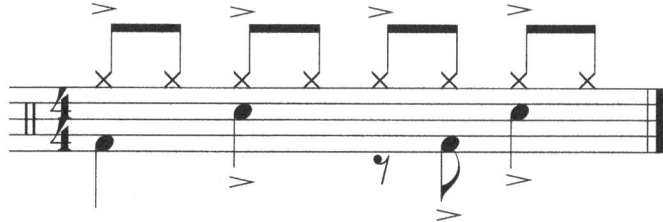

Drumset music employing "stems up" notation often contains two or more notes on a single stem. Whenever two or more instruments share a stem, articulations can be placed at the positions that offer the most clarity and readability.

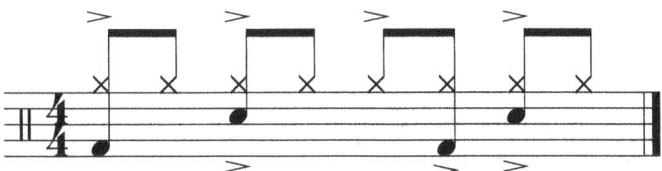

OPEN HI-HAT

It is recommended that the open hi-hat cymbals be written as an "X" notehead with an open circle articulation mark. If an open hi-hat is followed closely by a closed hi-hat played with a stick, it is not necessary to indicate a foot-played hi-hat. Indicate a foot-closed hi-hat only if that note is to sound without using a stick.

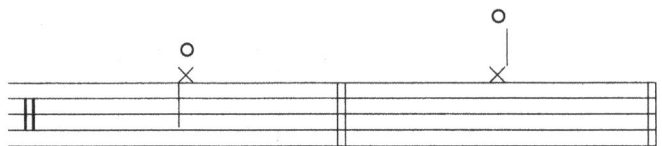

Foot-closed / Open Hi-hat

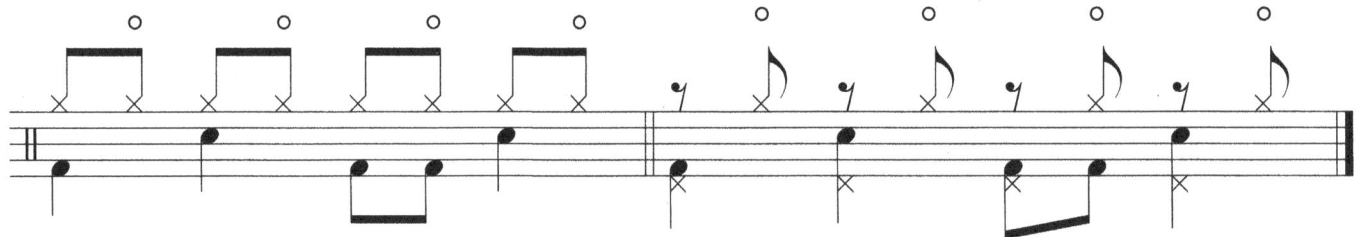

CLOSED HI-HAT

When necessary, closed hi-hat notes should be written with the articulation of the plus sign. However, the inclusion of circle and plus signs over every note would be cumbersome and clumsy. It should be assumed that all notes for the hi-hat are closed unless otherwise indicated. The articulation for the closed hi-hat should not be used unless the composer or arranger feels that its inclusion would clarify a particular passage.

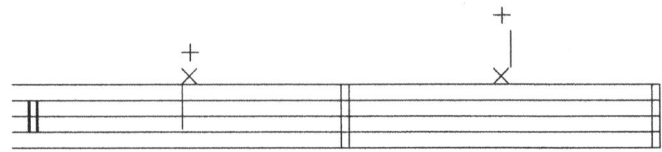

HALF-OPEN HI-HAT

The symbol of an open circle bisected by a line should be used to indicate a half-open (or half-closed) hi-hat. While this performance technique is not as commonly notated as the stroke for fully open hi-hats, it does offer a higher degree of precision and musical nuance.

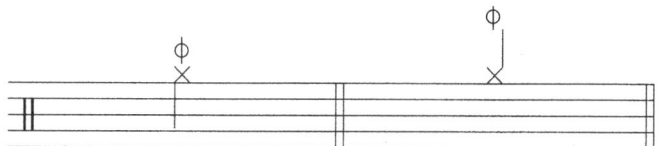

FOOT SPLASH

The foot-splash is a technique that involves playing the hi-hat pedal in such a manner as to create a sound similar to a pair of small crash cymbals, rather than the tight "chick" sound normally associated with the hi-hat cymbals played with the foot.

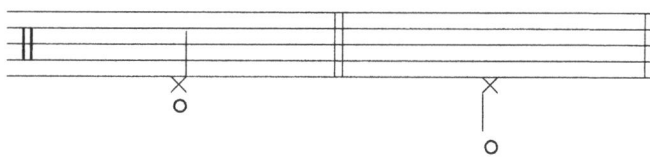

CLOSED HI-HAT WITH FOOT

It should be assumed that all notes for the foot-controlled hi-hat be closed unless otherwise indicated. The articulation symbol for the closed hi-hat played with the foot is the plus sign. This articulation should not be used unless the composer or arranger feels that its inclusion would clarify a particular passage.

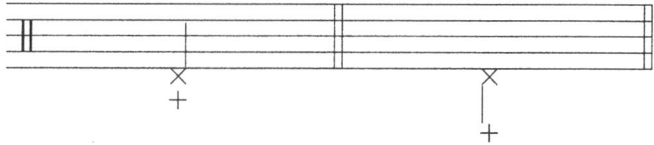

STOP VIBRATIONS

Notes on drums that are to be performed so that the natural vibrations are cut off should use the plus sign for such purposes. In contrast, the open circle can be used to indicate notes that are not stopped. These symbols should be used only if the passage would benefit from additional clarity. Otherwise, it can be assumed that a drum will be allowed to ring.

Stopped Drums

Open Drums

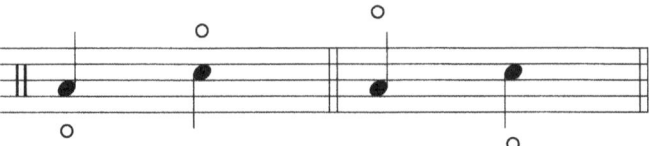

Open and Stopped Toms

A cymbal "choke" is performed by the player reaching up and grabbing the edge of the cymbal to stop the vibrations. The choke is indicated by an apostrophe.

Choked Cymbals

LET RING

It should be assumed that all instruments of the drumset will be allowed to ring for the entire length of their natural decay. It is recommended that composers and arrangers use the incomplete tie to indicate notes that are allowed to ring through their natural decay only if they feel that certain passages would benefit from this additional clarification. Otherwise, no special articulation or durational value is required.

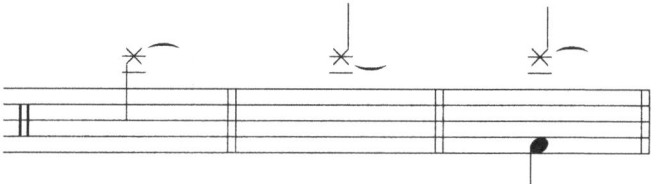

The direction of the tie depends upon the direction of the stem. In single-voice music, notes with downstems have the arc of the tie on top, and notes with upstems have the arc of the tie on the bottom. In two-voice music, this is generally reversed.

In drumset music, the Let Ring indication is most often used with cymbals, as a crash cymbal will generally be written in the same voice with the ride cymbal and/or hi-hat, and will be played with the same hand.

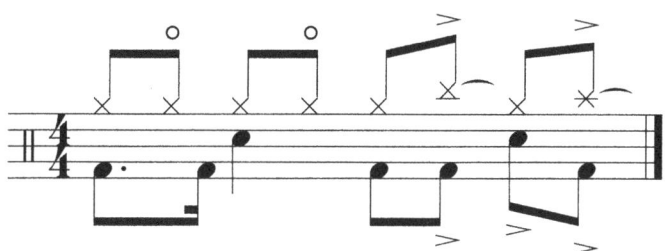

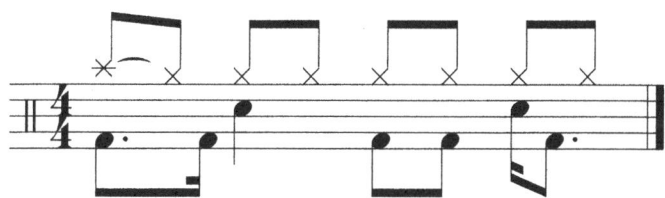

SURFACE-AREA INDICATIONS

While surface-area indications are more common in works written for multiple-percussion than for drumset, composers and arrangers may want to incorporate more accurate surface-area indications in the future. It is unnecessary to indicate any surface-area specification unless the composer or arranger is asking for a special musical effect.

If the use of a special surface area is desired, it is best indicated by a brief word or two written above the music (such as "bell," "edge" or "center"). If the indications of surface areas change so often that written text becomes cumbersome, an additional articulation mark may be included for clarity.

BELL AND EDGE OF CYMBAL

The bell can be indicated by a pictogram of a cymbal with a stick near the bell (dome) of the cymbal. When playing at the edge of the cymbal is to be specified, use a pictogram of a cymbal with a stick near the edge of the cymbal.

Bell of Cymbal

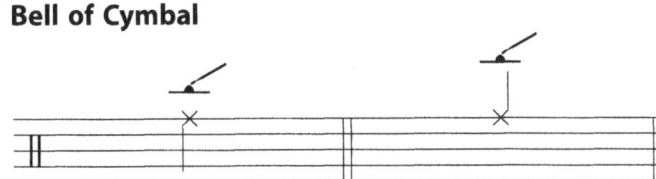

Edge of Cymbal

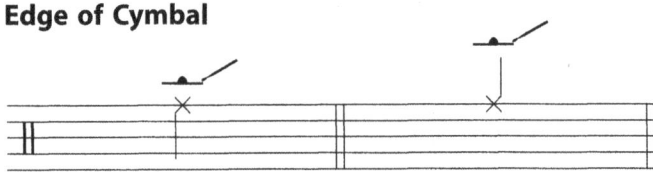

CENTER AND EDGE OF DRUM

The center or edge of the drum can be indicated by a pictogram of a circle representing the drumhead with an "x" at the desired striking area.

Center of Drum

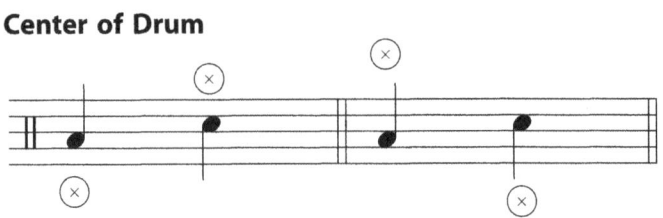

Edge of Drum

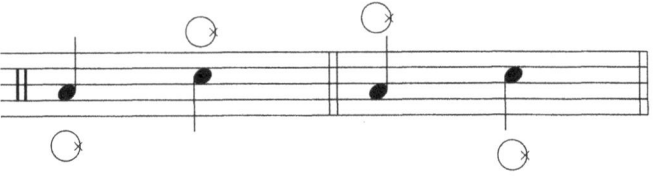

STICKING

This guideline recommends the use of the uppercase letters "R" and "L" for sticking indications. Sticking should not be included in the music unless the composer or arranger desires a specific sticking for a particular effect, or if the music is instructional in nature.

In single-voice music using upstem notation or in linear drumset notation in which there is only one note per stem, stickings should be placed below the staff. In two-voice notation, stickings can be placed above or below the staff to most clearly indicate the desired effect.

BEATERS

The use of special graphic symbols for beaters has been covered in a wide variety of books dealing with contemporary percussion notation. It is recommended that beaters be indicated by written instruction unless the composer or arranger feels that fast changes between a number of different beaters would be better understood by graphic symbols. If graphic symbols are to be used, they should be defined in the key, and their use should be strictly observed throughout the publication.

The graphic symbol for a brush should be a pictogram of a brush. The symbol for soft mallets should be an open (non-filled) circle at the end of a vertical line, the symbol for a hard mallet should be a solid (filled) circle at the end of a vertical line, and the symbol for a medium-hard mallet should be a half-filled circle at the end of a vertical line. The symbol for a normal drumstick should consist of a pictogram of a drumstick or a very small closed circle at the end of a vertical line. Esoteric beaters (such as knitting needles, rattan sticks, Superballs or coins, to name a few) can be indicated by a brief word in the score or defined as a graphic symbol in the key.

Drum Stick   Brush   Hard Mallet   Soft Mallet   Medium Mallet

WRITTEN INSTRUCTIONS

As English is becoming the international language of music, it is the recommendation of this guideline that all written instructions be given in English, or that they include an English translation. Instructions that are longer than a few words should be given a special symbol or short descriptive word and defined as such in the legend. It is cumbersome to include long passages of descriptive text in close relation to the staff. All written instructions should appear above the staff.

ADDITIONAL ARTICULATIONS

Hundreds of different timbres can be coaxed from the drumset by the use of special mallets and performance techniques combined with various surface areas. It would be impossible to codify every possible request from every composer, as innovative ideas for creating new sounds are constantly being devised.

When additional performance techniques are necessary (such as playing on the shell of a drum or rimshot variations), they should be fully explained in the legend and indicated in the score with brief text. If the alterations and modifications occur so often as to make the use of text cumbersome, additional articulations can be devised. When new articulations must be created to define a particular performance technique, they should be clearly defined in the legend and strictly adhered to throughout the entire publication.

It is further recommended that normal musical symbols for articulation and expression (accent, marcato, tenuto, staccato and their combinations) be avoided for the purpose of creating special drumset articulations. In addition, individual or unconventional abbreviations should not be used for this purpose. Instead, composers and arrangers may be free to invent their own signs, or use special articulation symbols normally associated with non-percussion instruments or techniques.

6
VOICING

It is recommended that all drumset music be written in one or two voices, depending on the musical context and the voicing that will provide the clearest intentions of the composer or arranger. Following general notational practices, when two lines of music are written on the same staff, the stems for the upper voice are upstems while the stems for the lower voice are downstems, regardless of their position on the staff.

Generally speaking, passages that are often called "time patterns" contain one or more instruments that perform an ostinato or rhythmically simple passages, and one or more instruments that play a rhythmic figure of more complexity and freedom. This type of playing is also called "vertical," as two or more instruments often play at the same time. These passages are best notated in two voices.

Two Voices

Passages that can be described as fills or solos are often best notated as a single voice. Single-voice notation is also preferred for a drumming style called "linear." In linear drumming, two instruments rarely sound together.

One Voice

Certain musical situations are less clear. The examples below illustrate how the same measure could be written using one or two voices. The composer or arranger should decide which notation is most legible. In the examples below, most drummers would prefer the second versions, as the roles of the different limbs are more clearly defined.

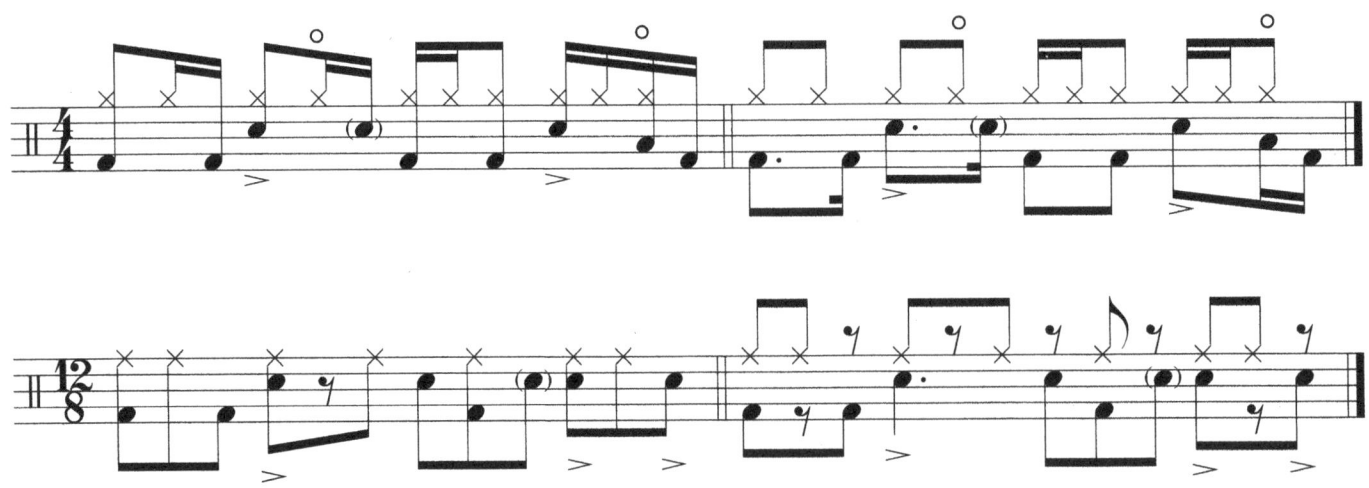

VOICING • 29

When notating beat patterns in two-voice music, the snare drum can either be part of the ride cymbal/hi-hat voice, or part of the bass drum voice, depending on which seems more clear in a given situation. The snare drum should not migrate between two voices within the same measure, however.

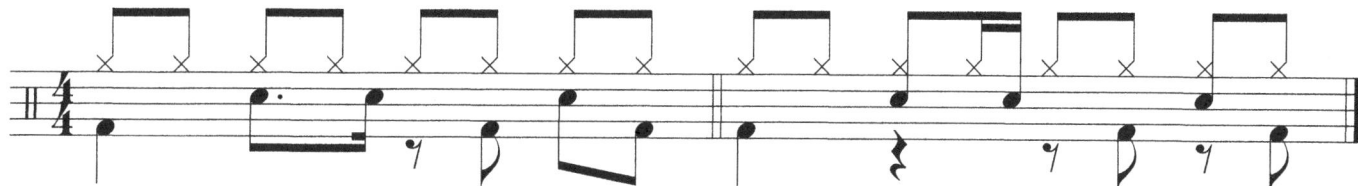

It can be appropriate to change between two-voice and one-voice textures if the nature of the part is changing. For example, a drummer might go from a timekeeping pattern that would typically be notated in two-voice format to a fill or solo line that is played and notated in a linear fashion.

PLACEMENT OF RESTS

All two-voice drumset notation must contain the rests necessary to ensure that both voices are complete. The position of rests placed upon the staff can be shifted so that it is clear to what line the rest belongs.

Incorrect   Correct

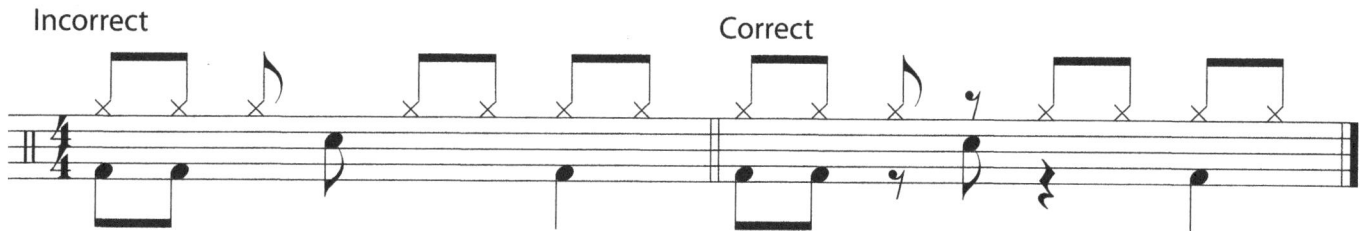

However, if both parts contain a common rest, the rest can be written once at its normal staff location.

Acceptable   Better

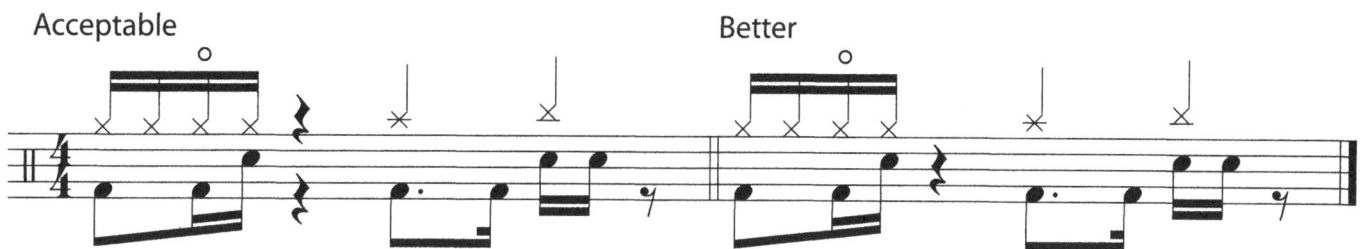

7
LEGEND

The legend (also called a "notation key" or simply "key") is a graphic explanation of the notation system used by the composer or arranger. This guideline recommends the following concerning a legend:

1. All compositions and charts should include a legend.

2. The legend should be given before any actual music is indicated in the work. The legend may be presented during the introductory text in a method book, the first staff system in an improvisational-style chart, or above the music in an article included in a journal or magazine.

3. The legend should include the staff positions for all instruments (written with their associated noteheads), all articulation signs (other than standard accents, staccato marks, etc.), all beater signs and all additional notational graphic symbols used in the music.

4. All symbols, staff positions, notehead alterations, sticking, beaters, etc, must be consistent throughout the entire publication or section of the publication.

5. Do not include any notation signs or symbols in the music that are not defined in the legend, other than the standard musical symbols of accents, staccato marks, etc. Do not define any notation signs or symbols in the legend that are not required in the music.

6. The only allowable addition to the music after the legend is given should be written text.

Following are examples of typical legends, ranging from basic and simple to very detailed.

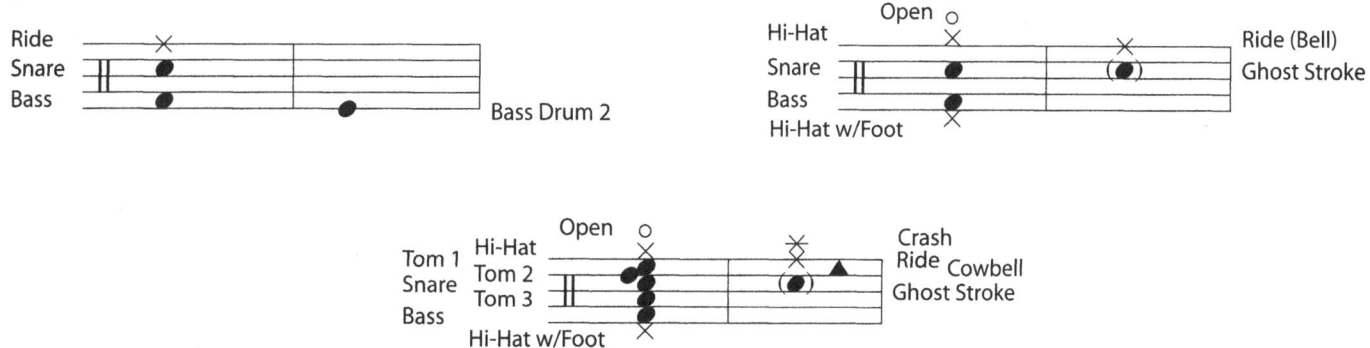

32 • Guide to Standardized Drumset Notation

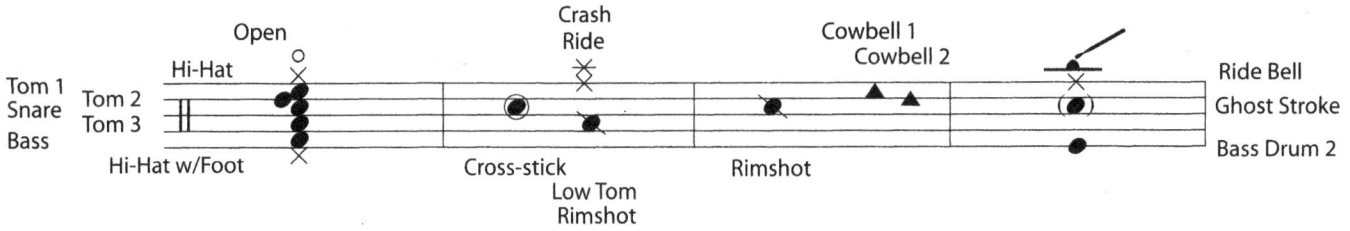

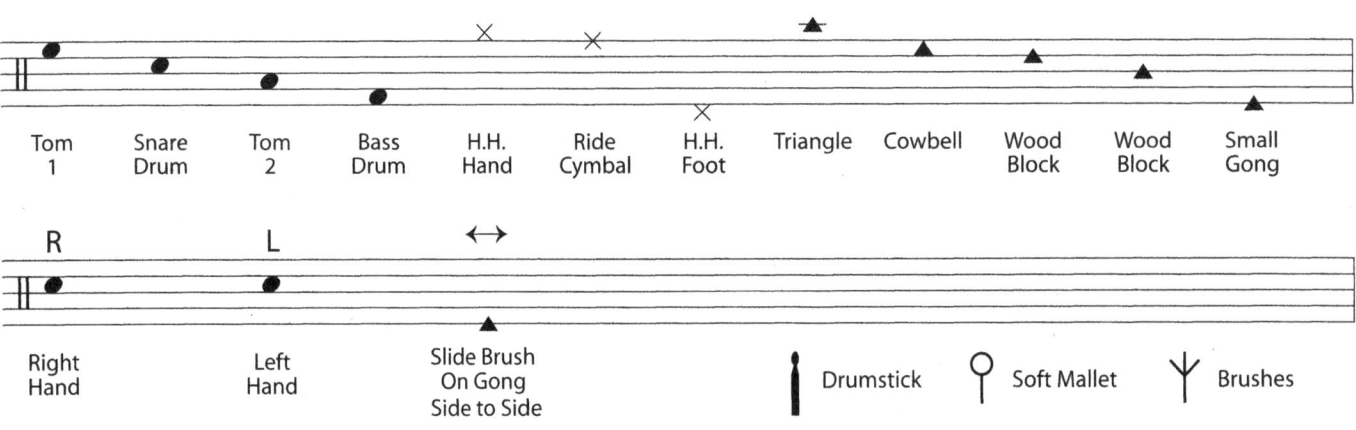

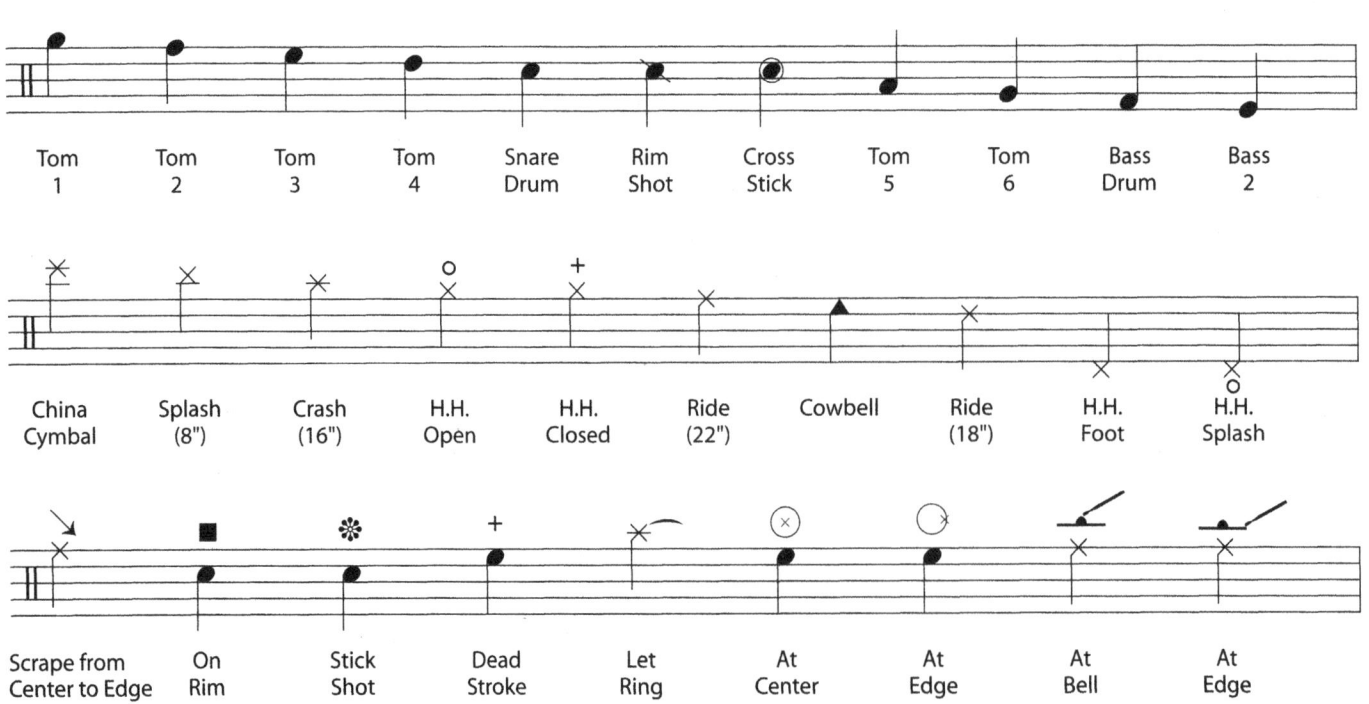

8
IMPROVISATIONAL NOTATION

WRITTEN BEATS

Composers and arrangers should always provide the drumset player with a simplified version of a stylistically correct time pattern at the style's first appearance. If desired, the term "ad lib." can be written above the basic beat pattern to indicate creative freedom. If all composers and arrangers provided this basic service for drummers, younger players would be able to sight-read a basic time pattern that was stylistically correct, while experienced players would be more creative, as the "ad lib." indication clearly shows the composer's intent.

The musical examples below are only illustrative of this recommendation. They are by no means the only stylistically correct time patterns for a given style of music. It is, of course, the responsibilty of the composer, arranger, editor, and publisher to include basic time styles that would complement the music.

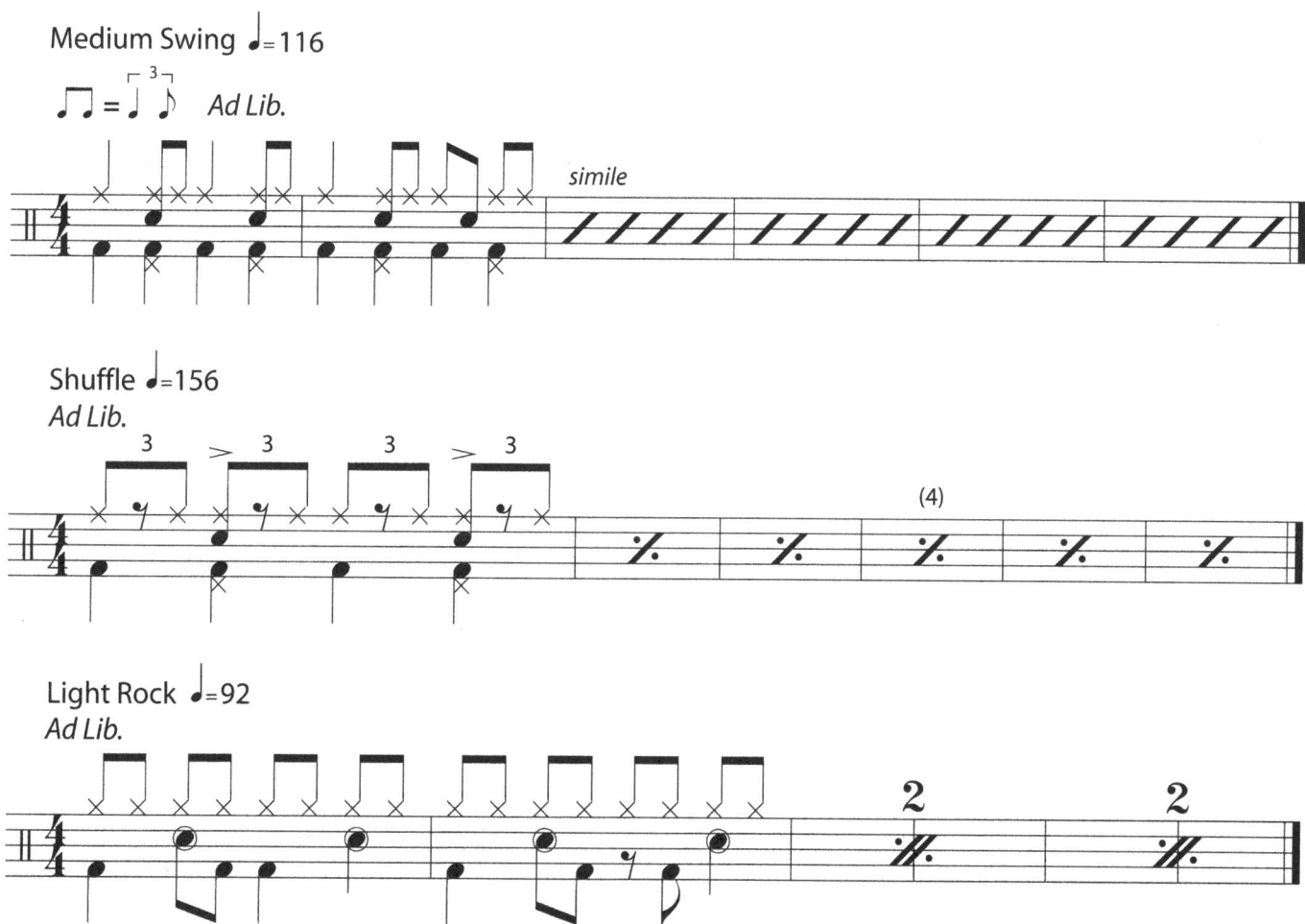

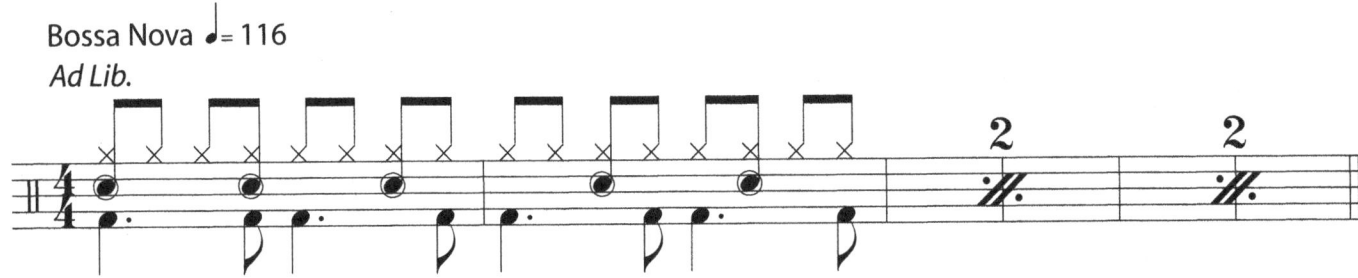

TIME STYLES

A precisely written beat pattern should be used whenever exact parts are desired or if the performer is to play certain rhythms exactly as written. In such cases, the composer or arranger may choose to add indications such as "As written," "Bass drum as written," "Hi-hat as written," etc., for additional clarity. If these written indications are not added to the music, the performer should feel free to play (or not play) the notated passage.

If the performer is free to improvise all parts, a series of one-bar repeats or slash measures can be used. It is assumed that composers and arrangers will want to use both methods of time notation, depending on what is more clear and better suits their needs.

Time Pattern As Written

Time Pattern With Variation

Free Repeats

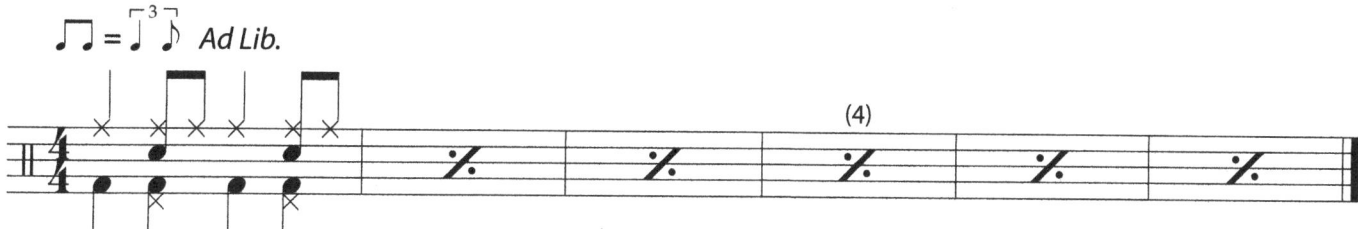

Free Slash

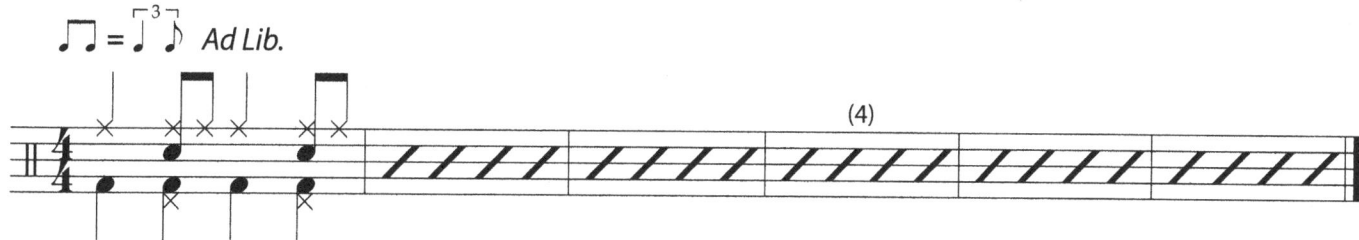

The multi-measure rest should NEVER be used to indicate that a musican is to continue playing time. If space is at a premium and a series of individual measures with repeats or slashes is not possible or practical, one of the following time notation options may be used.

Time Option 1

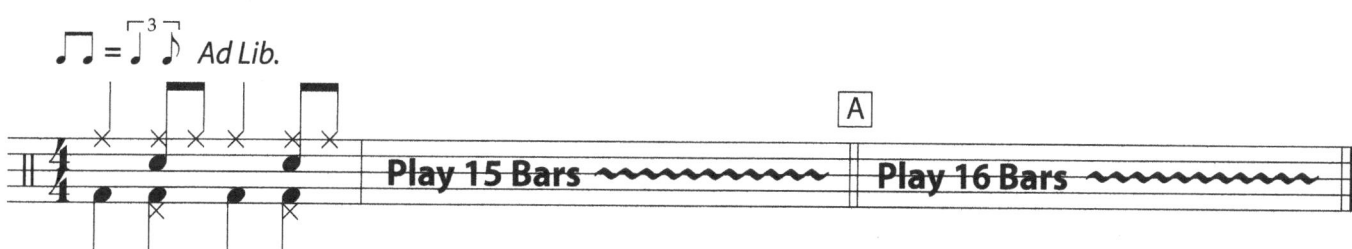

Time Option 2

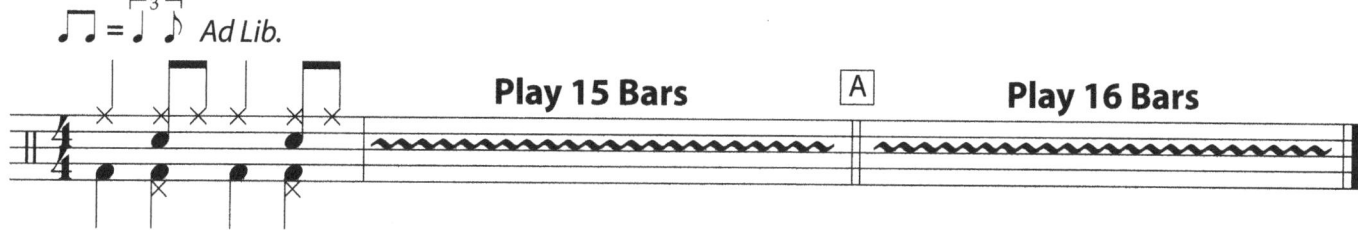

FILLS AND SOLOS

It is recommended that the instruction "Solo" be used only when the performer is featured for the specified length of time. Similar to the use of the term in orchestral parts, "Solo" indicates that no other instruments in the ensemble are playing, or that the part is to stand out from the remaining instruments in the ensemble.

Solo Section

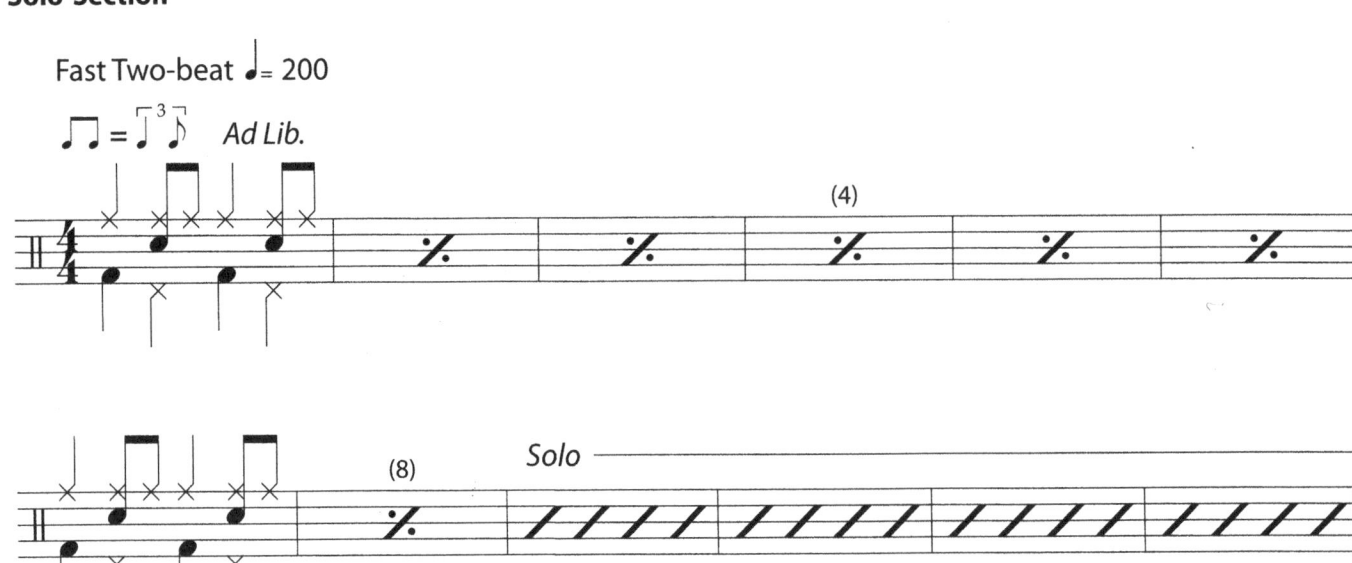

The term "Fill" is much less specific, and should be used for all indications that are not solos.

There are three common types of solos and fills—those that are precisely notated, those that are rhythmically precise without indicating the exact instrument, and those that are improvised.

PRECISELY NOTATED FILLS OR SOLOS

Obviously, precise fills or solos should be notated exactly as the composer wishes them to sound. So there can be no question that the performer is to play the written notes, the instruction "as written" should be included above the fill or solo.

Precise Solo

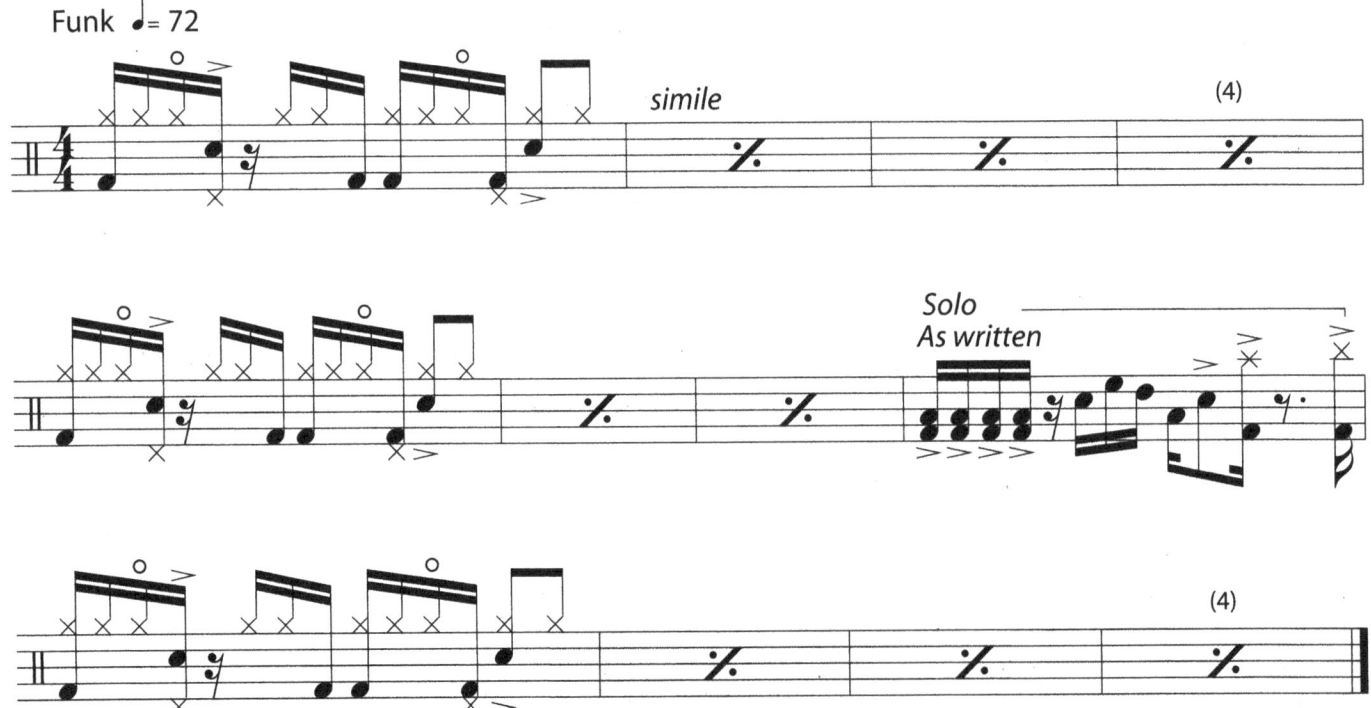

IMPROVISATIONAL NOTATION • 37

Precise Fill

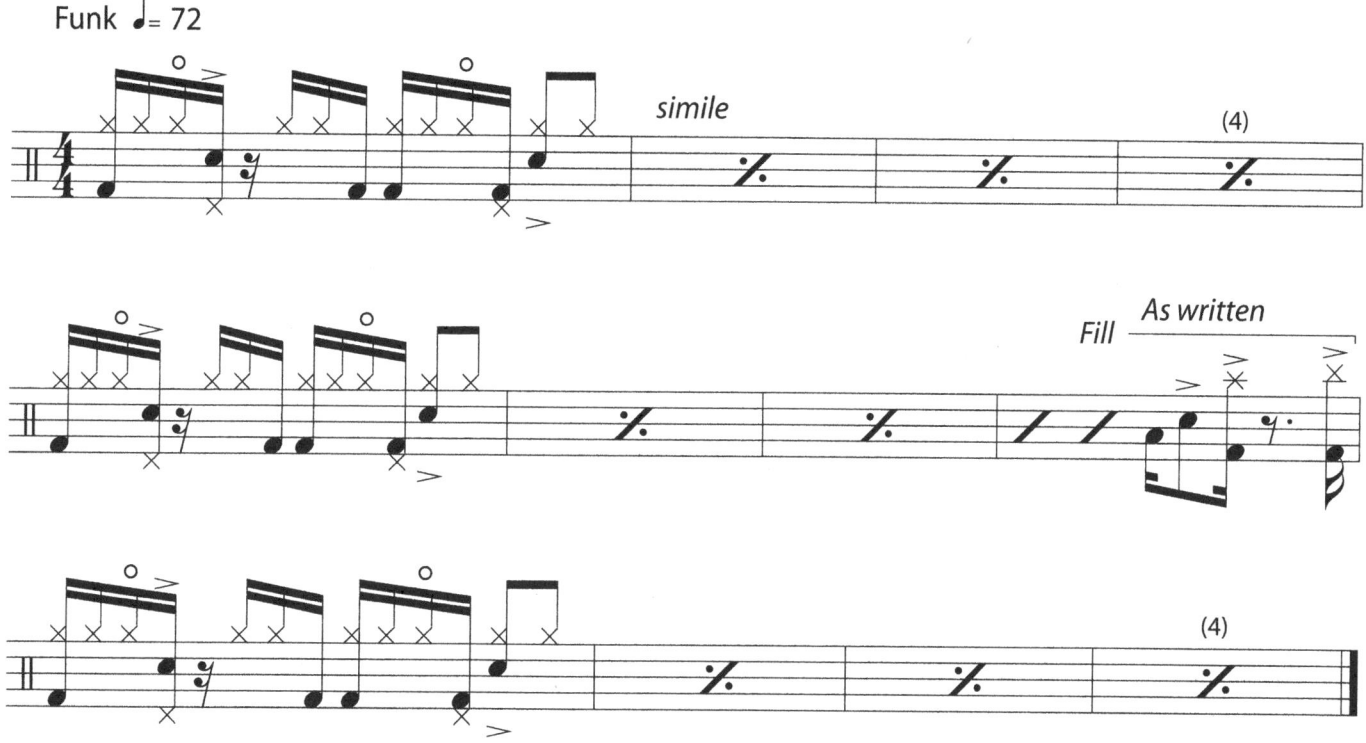

RHYTHMICALLY NOTATED FILLS OR SOLOS
Fills and solos that notate the rhythm, but not the instruments, should be written with slashed noteheads on the middle line of the staff.

Rhythmic Solo

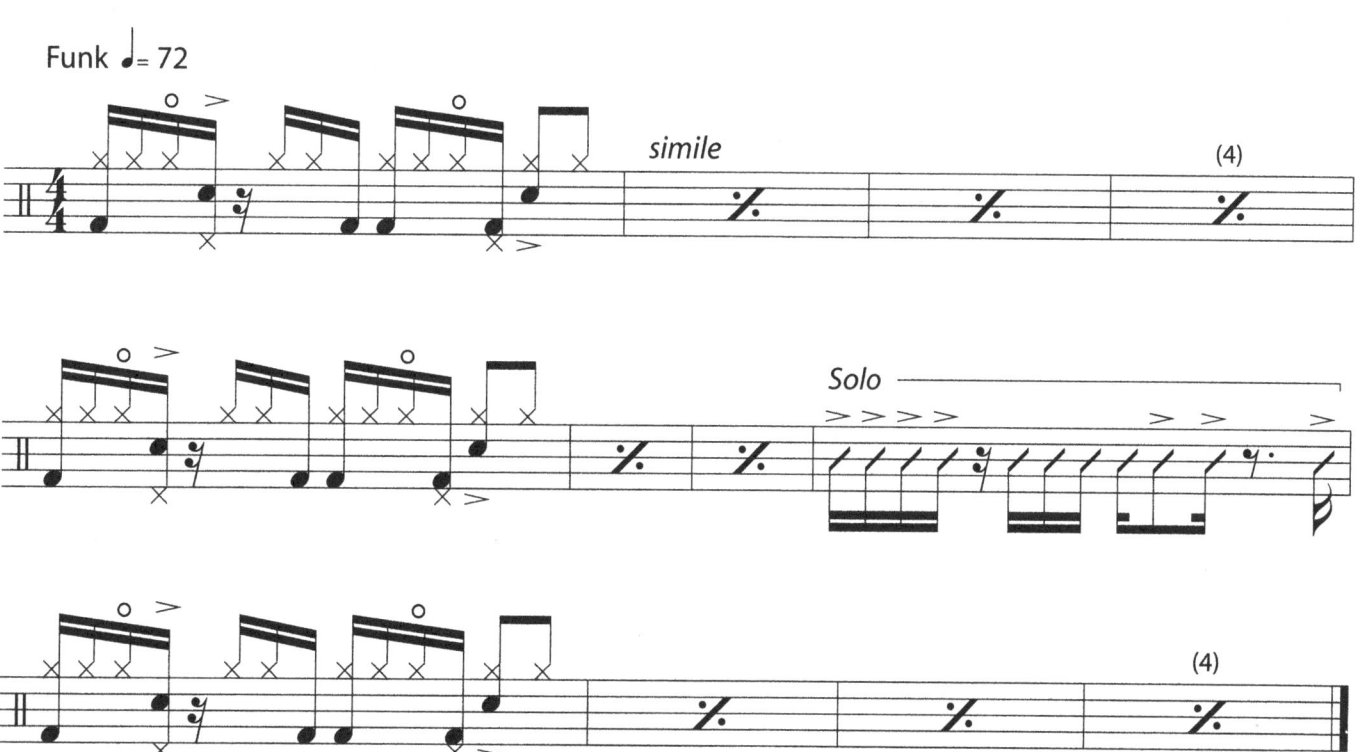

Rhythmic Fill

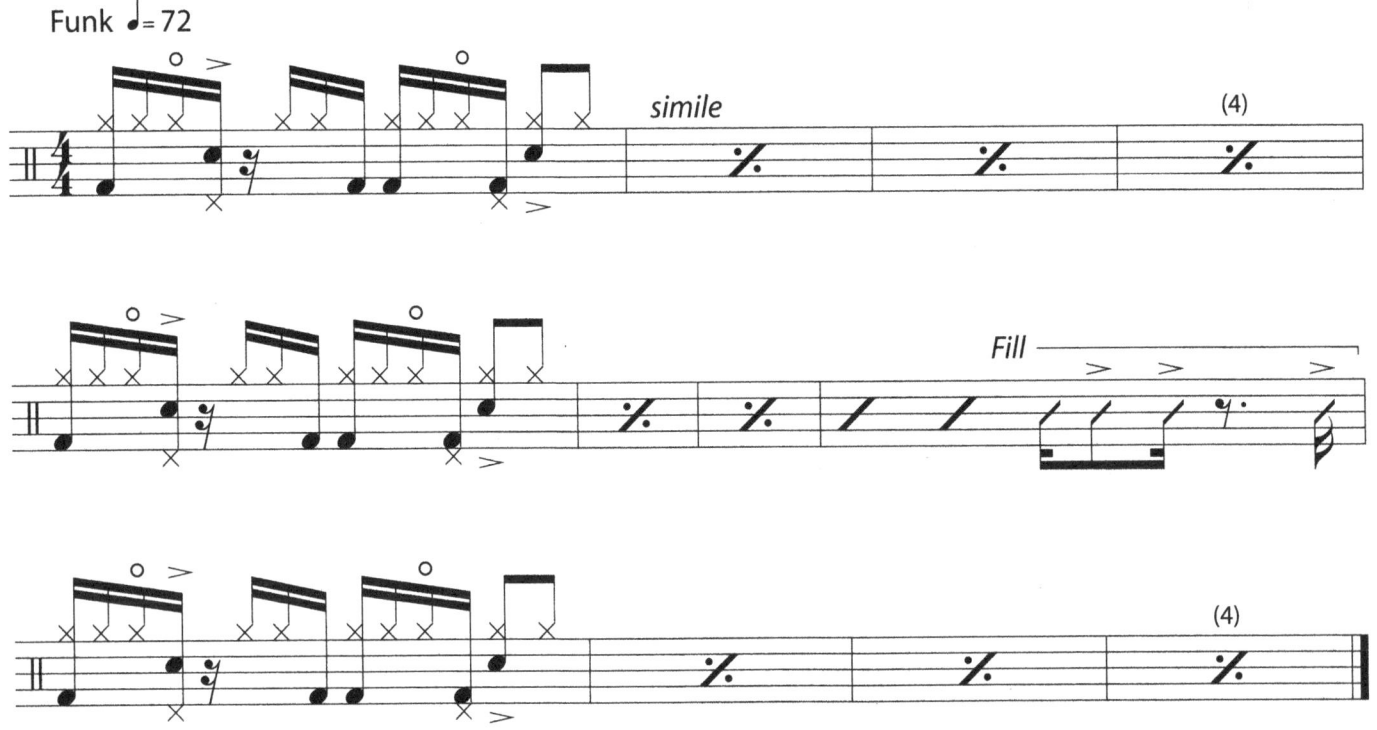

IMPROVISED FILLS OR SOLOS

Slash notation should be used to indicate improvised solos or fills.

Free Solo

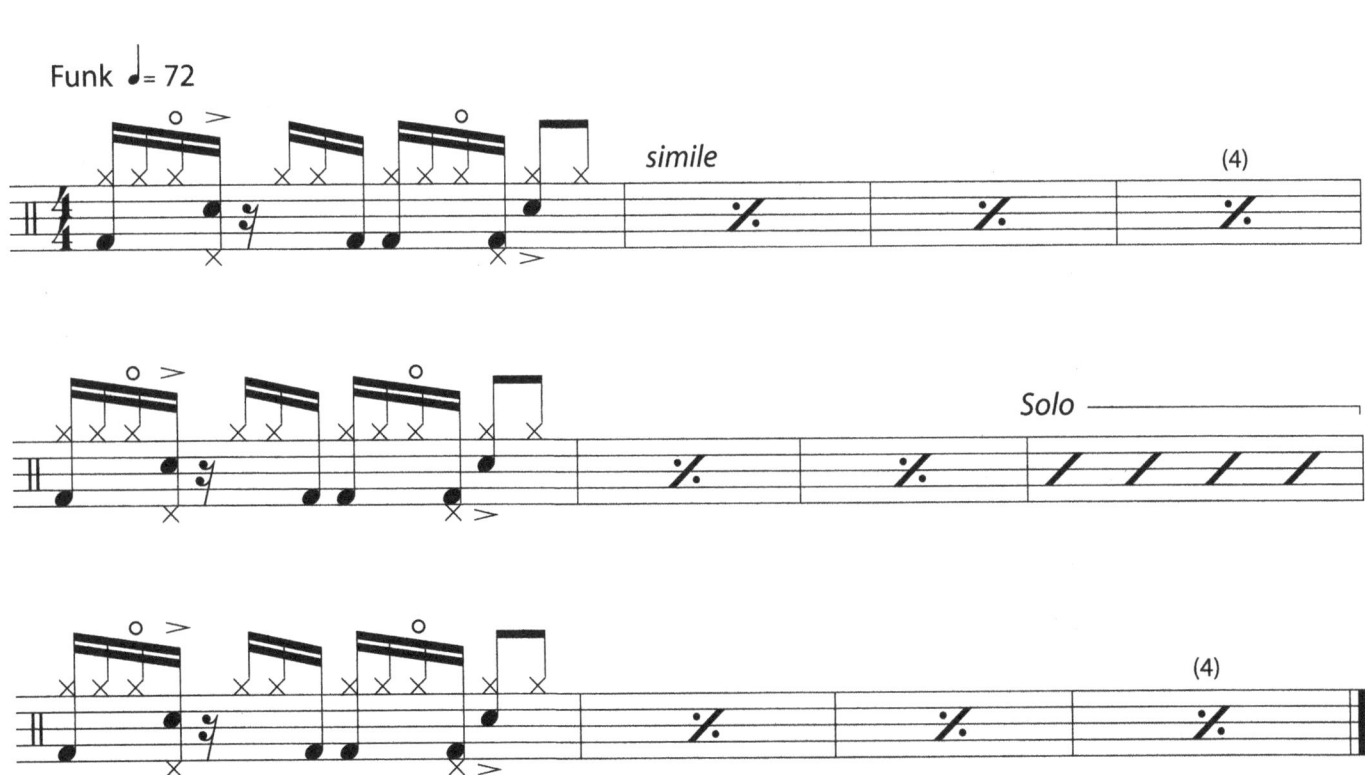

Free Fill

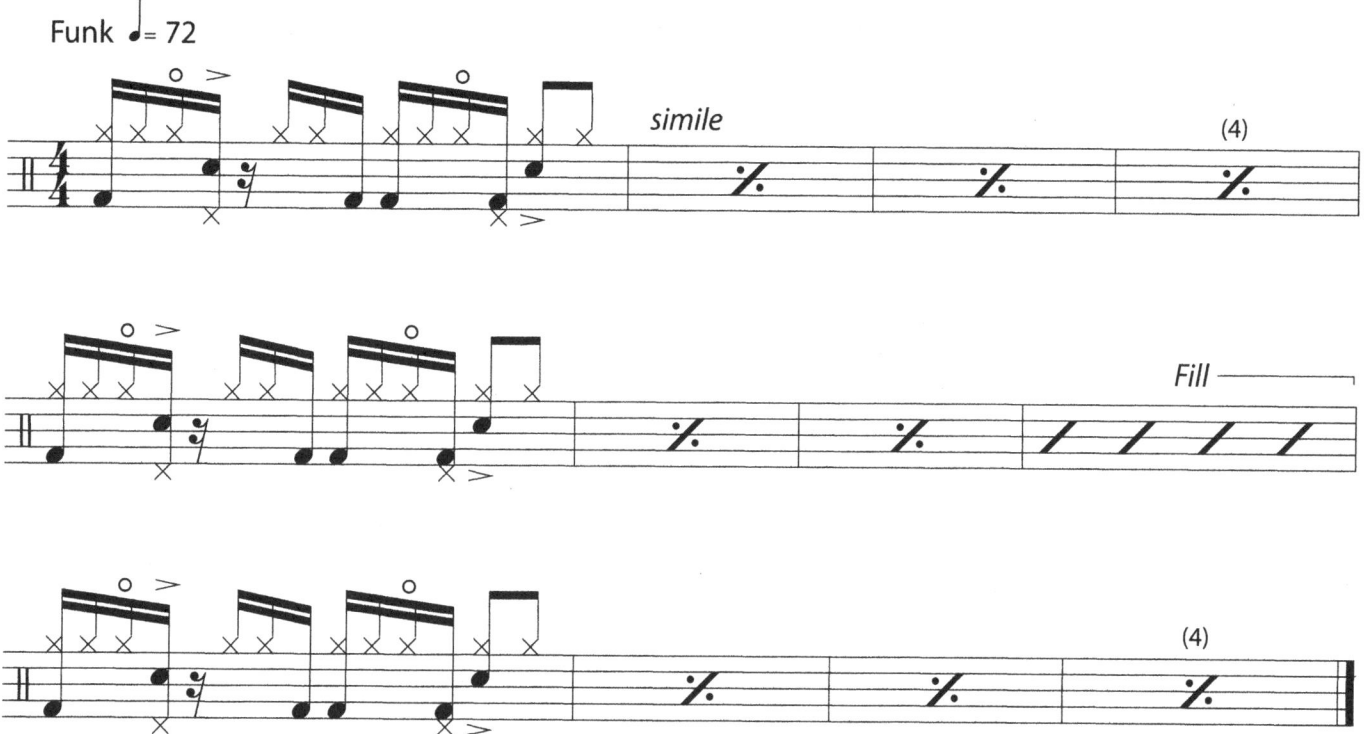

SECTION/ENSEMBLE FIGURES

It is recommended that all section and ensemble figures (rhythms played by other instruments that the drummer is expected to reinforce) be written above the staff in cue-size notes. When such figures are written in cue-size notes above the staff, their meaning is clear. It would be difficult to interpret section/ensemble figures as rhythms for any specific instrument in the drumset.

In addition, it is recommended that all section/ensemble figures include a written indication that identifies the instrument or section performing the rhythm. This knowledge is vital to an intelligent, musical decision concerning how the performer will interpret the figure on the drumset.

STRUCTURAL INDICATIONS

In "road map"-style drum charts that have little actual music and that are designed primarily to aid the drummer in following the formal structure of the tune, composers or arrangers can be extremely helpful by providing written indications such as "Intro," "Guitar Solo" "Sax Tutti" "Vamp," etc.

BIBLIOGRAPHY

Avgerinos, Gerassimos. *Handbuch der Schlag- und Effektinstrumente*. Frankfurt: Verlag Das Musikinstrument, 1967.

Boehm, Lasslo. *Modern Music Notation: A Reference and Textbook*. New York: G. Schirmer, 1961.

Brindle, Reginald Smith. *Contemporary Percussion*. London: Oxford University Press, 1970.

Caskel, Cristoph. "Notation for Percussion Instruments." Translated by Vernon Martin. *Percussionist* 8 (March 1971): 80–84.

Chew, Geoffrey. "Notation." *The New Grove Dictionary of Music and Musicians*. Vol. X. Edited by Stanley Sadie. London: Macmillian, 1980. XX.

Cole, Hugo. *Sounds and Signs: Aspects of Musical Notation*. London: Oxford University Press, 1974.

Cope, David. *New Music Notation*. Dubuque, IA: Kendall/Hunt Pub. Co., 1976.

Gaburo, Virginia. *Notation (a lecture to be performed by solo speaker to attentive audience)*. La Jolla, CA: Lingua Press, 1977.

Gerou, Tom, and Linda Lusk. *Essential Dictionary of Music Notation*. Los Angeles, Alfred Publishing Co. Inc., 1996.

Gieseler, Walter, Luca Lombardi, and Rold-Dieter Weyer. *Instrumentation in der Musik des 20. Jahrhunderts*. Celle: Moeck Verlag, 1985.

Heussenstamm, George. *The Norton Manual of Music Notation*. New York: W. W. Norton & Co., 1987.

Karkoschka, Erhard. *Notation in New Music*. Translated by Ruth Koenig. New York: Praeger Publishers, 1972.

Kotonski, Wlodzimier. *Schlaginstrumente in Modernen Orchester*. Mainz: B. Schott's Söhne, 1968.

McCarty, Frank. "Percussion Notation." *Percussionist* 15 (Winter 1978): 49–60.

_____. "Symbols for Percussion Notation." *Percussionist* 18 (Fall 1980): 8–19.

O'Neill, John C. "Recent Trends in Percussion Notation." *Percussionist* 18 (Fall 1980) 20–55.

Peinkofer, Karl and Fritz Tannigel. *Handbook of Percussion Instruments*. Translated by Kurt Stone and Else Stone. London: Schott, 1969.

Percussive Arts Society. *Standardization of Percussion Notation*. Terre Haute, IN: Percussive Arts Society, 1973.

Peters, Gordon B. "Outline Guide to Percussion Notation." *Instrumentalist* 20 (June 1966): 69–72.

"Project on Terminology and Notation of Percussion Instruments." by Gordon Peters, Chairman. *Percussionist* 3 (April 1966):47–53.

Rastall, Richard. *The Notation of Western Music: An Introduction*. London: J. M. Dent & Sons Ltd., 1983.

Read, Gardner. *Music Notation*. New York: Crescendo Books, 1978.

⎯⎯⎯⎯. *Source Book of Proposed Music Notation Reforms*. Music Reference Series, no. 11. Westport, CT: Greenwood Press, 1987.

Risatti, Howard. *New Music Vocabulary: A Guide to Notational Signs for Contemporary Music*. Urbana: University of Illinois Press, 1975.

Roemer, Clinton. *The Art of Music Copying: The Preparation of Music for Performance*. 2d ed. Sherman Oaks, CA: Roerick Music Co., 1985.

Sabbe, Herman, Kurt Stone, and Gerald Warfield, eds. "International Conference on New Musical Notation Report." *Interface* 4 (November 1975): 1–120.

Stone, Kurt. *Music Notation in the Twentieth Century: A Practical Guidebook*. New York: W. W. Norton & Co., 1980.

Udow, Michael W. "Visual Correspondence Between Notation Systems and Instrument Configurations." *Percussive Notes* 18 (Winter 1981): 15–29.

Warfield, Gerald. *How to Write Music Manuscript (In Pencil); A Workbook in the Basics of Music Notation*. New York: D. McKay Co., 1977.

ABOUT THE AUTHOR

Norman Weinberg is Director of Percussion Studies at The University of Arizona. He has performed as Principal Timpanist with the Corpus Christi Symphony Orchestra, the Jerusalem Symphony Orchestra, the Evansville Philharmonic, the Spoleto Festival Orchestra and the Leonard Bernstein Festival Orchestra, and has been Professor of Music at Del Mar College in Corpus Christi, Texas.

He has been involved with electronic percussion instruments for several years, and has been awarded four grants to research the viability of using electronic percussion instruments as a teaching tool. He has presented seminars at many regional and national conventions including the Texas Music Educators Association Convention, The Texas Association of Music Schools Convention, the Ontario "Celebration of the Drum," the Day of Percussion Festivals in Oklahoma, Texas and Utah, the Phi Mu Alpha Sinfonia National Convention, and two Percussive Arts Society International Conventions (PASIC).

A prolific author, Weinberg is an Associate Editor for *Percussive Notes*, and has published over one hundred articles in journals including *Modern Drummer, Drum!, Drums and Drumming, Rhythm, Percussive Notes, Percussive Notes Research Edition, Keyboard Magazine, EQ Magazine, The Instrumentalist* and *Home Recording Newsletter*. In addition, he has several compositions published by Southern Music Corporation. His book *The Electronic Drummer* is published by Modern Drummer Publications and is distributed by Hal Leonard Corporation.

Weinberg was awarded the prestigious Performer's Certificate from Indiana University, where he received the Master of Music degree in Percussion Performance with Honors, and the Doctor of Music Arts degree. He is a Yamaha Performing Artist, a Zildjian Educational Clinician and endorses Innovative Percussion Mallets.

Weinberg created and helped to establish the PAS World Percussion Network (WPN — http://www.pas.org). This is an electronic database of information related to percussion performance, research, education, and literature, available on the Internet. At PASIC '94, Weinberg received the Outstanding Service Award from the Percussive Arts Society.